The
Unofficial
DISNEY PARKS
COOKBOOK

Your Guide to the Happiest Kitchen on Earth!

The Unofficial DISNEY PARKS COOKBOOK

From Delicious *Dole Whip* to Tasty *Mickey Pretzels,*
100 Magical Disney-Inspired Recipes

ASHLEY CRAFT

Adams Media

New York • London • Toronto • Sydney • New Delhi

Adams Media
An Imprint of Simon & Schuster, Inc.
100 Technology Center Drive
Stoughton, MA 02072

Copyright © 2020 by Ashley Craft.

All rights reserved, including the right to reproduce this book or portions thereof in any form whatsoever. For information address Adams Media Subsidiary Rights Department, 1230 Avenue of the Americas, New York, NY 10020.

First Adams Media hardcover edition November 2020

ADAMS MEDIA and colophon are trademarks of Simon & Schuster.

For information about special discounts for bulk purchases, please contact Simon & Schuster Special Sales at 1-866-506-1949 or business@simonandschuster.com.

The Simon & Schuster Speakers Bureau can bring authors to your live event. For more information or to book an event contact the Simon & Schuster Speakers Bureau at 1-866-248-3049 or visit our website at www.simonspeakers.com.

Interior design by Sylvia McArdle
Interior photographs by Harper Point Photography
Interior illustrations by Alaya Howard

Manufactured in China

10 9 8 7 6 5 4 3 2 1

Library of Congress Cataloging-in-Publication Data
Names: Craft, Ashley, author.
Title: The unofficial Disney parks cookbook / Ashley Craft.
Description: Avon, Massachusetts: Adams Media, 2020. | Series: Unofficial cookbook. | Includes index.
Identifiers: LCCN 2020034530 | ISBN 9781507214510 (hc) | ISBN 9781507214527 (ebook)
Subjects: LCSH: Disney, Walt, 1901–1966. | Cooking--California--Disneyland. | Disneyland (Calif.) | LCGFT: Cookbooks.
Classification: LCC TX715.2.C34 C73 2020 | DDC 641.59794--dc23
LC record available at https://lccn.loc.gov/2020034530

ISBN 978-1-5072-1451-0
ISBN 978-1-5072-1452-7 (ebook)

Many of the designations used by manufacturers and sellers to distinguish their products are claimed as trademarks. Where those designations appear in this book and Simon & Schuster, Inc., was aware of a trademark claim, the designations have been printed with initial capital letters.

Many of the designations used in this book, including but not limited to place names and character names, are the registered trademarks of The Walt Disney Company. Where those designations appear in the book and the publisher was aware of the trademark status, the designations have been printed with initial capital letters.

Always follow safety and commonsense cooking protocols while using kitchen utensils, operating ovens and stoves, and handling uncooked food. If children are assisting in the preparation of any recipe, they should always be supervised by an adult.

Dedication

For Danny, my forever taste tester.

Contents

Preface 14

Introduction 16

PART 1

DISNEY PARKS COOKING 101 18

CHAPTER 1

The Delicious Disney Experience 21

CHAPTER 2

The Disney Cook's Essentials. 33

PART 2

MAGICAL RECIPES . . .46

CHAPTER 3

Disneyland 49

Churros 53

Raspberry Rose Mickey Macarons. 54

Cookies and Cream Mickey Cupcakes 57

Bengal Beef Skewers 60

Jungle Juleps 61

Tiger Tail Breadsticks 62

Hummus Trio 63

Pork Belly Skewers 65

Safari Skewers 66

Beignets. 67

Fritters 70

Clam Chowder. 71

Mint Juleps. 72

Gold Port Galley Lemonade 74

Churro Funnel Cake. 75

The Grey Stuff Gâteau 76

Matterhorn Macaroons 78

Brownie Bites 79

CHAPTER 4

Magic Kingdom 81

Mickey Sugar Cookies 85

Caramel Apples 86

Bacon Macaroni & Cheese
Hot Dogs 87

Corn Dog Nuggets 88

Sweet-and-Spicy Chicken Waffle
Sandwiches 89

Funnel Cake 91

Fresh Fruit Waffle Sandwiches . . 93

Cheshire Cat Tails 94

LeFou's Brew 96

The Grey Stuff 97

Gaston's Giant Cinnamon
Rolls 99

Peter Pan Floats 101	Croque Glacé 119
Tomato Basil Soup. 102	Napoleons 121
Turkey Legs. 103	Crêpes 123
Loaded Buffalo Chicken Tots 104	Tarte aux Fraises. 124
Cheeseburger Spring Rolls. . . . 106	School Bread 127
Pizza Spring Rolls 107	Troll Horns 128
Dole Whip 109	Caramel Popcorn 131
Pineapple Upside Down Cake. 110	Chocolate-Caramel Pineapple Spears. 132
Maple Popcorn 111	Caramel Pecan Bars. 133

CHAPTER 5

EPCOT 113

Croissant Doughnuts 117	
Macaron Ice Cream Sandwiches 118	Cocco Gelato. 141

Bavarian Cheesecake 134

Strawberry Kakigōri. 136

Melon Kakigōri 137

Mango Popsicles 139

Coconut Popsicles. 140

Stracciatella Gelato 143

Baklava 144

CHAPTER 6

Disney's Hollywood Studios. 147

Candy Apples 151

Perfect Popcorn 152

Carrot Cake Cookies 153

Butterfinger Cupcakes 154

Pretzels with Cream Cheese
Filling 156

Mickey Pretzels 158

Chocolate-Hazelnut Lunch Box
Tarts 161

Lemon-Blueberry Lunch Box
Tarts 162

Green Milk 163

Blue Milk 165

Outpost Popcorn Mix 166

Ronto Wraps 169

Peanut Butter and Jelly
Milk Shakes 171

Frozen Chocolate-Covered
Bananas 173

CHAPTER 7

Disney's Animal Kingdom . 175

Mickey Waffles 178

Haystacks 179

Night Blossoms 180

Cheeseburger Steamed Pods . . 182

Blueberry Cream Cheese
Mousse 185

Pongu Lumpia 188

Mr. Kamal's Seasoned Fries . . . 189

Frozen Lemonade 190

Mickey Ice Cream Sandwiches . 193

Mickey Ice Cream Bars 194

French Fries with Pulled Pork
and Cheese 195

Baked Macaroni & Cheese with
Pulled Pork 196

Baked Lobster Macaroni
& Cheese 199

CHAPTER 8

Disney California Adventure 201

Mangonada Smoothies 205

Carnitas Tacos 206

Berry Schmoozies 208

Churro Toffee 209

Pumpkin Spice Churros 210

Campfire Chili 211

S'mores 212

Cobbler Shakes 213

Corn Dogs 215

Chicken Drumsticks 216

Chili-Lime Corn on the Cob . . . 217

Jack-Jack's Num Num Cookies . 218

Pixar Pier Frosty Parfaits 221

Señor Buzz's Caliente Churros . 222

Bavarian Pretzels 223

Sally's Summer Churros 225

Standard US/Metric
Measurement Conversions . . . 227

Index 229

Acknowledgments

First, I have to thank my husband and best friend, Danny, for believing that I could publish this book and for supporting my Disney addiction all these years. Thanks to Elliot, Hazel, and Clifford (my kids) for bearing all the Disney Parks trips.

A major shout-out to my mother-in-law, Tricia Craft, dear friend Emily Goodsell, and Danny for being my "unofficial" editors and helping me hash out my first, second, and third drafts.

Thank you to my parents, Karen and Jeff Peterson, for their unending love and for buying the first copies of this book.

And I cannot forget my agent, Joe Perry. He is amazingly attentive and patient. Here's to many more projects together.

Finally, thank you to Julia and Adams Media for signing me for my first book and making me an author.

Preface

I was lucky enough to grow up in Anaheim Hills, California, just fifteen minutes from the Disneyland Resort. My family would sometimes say, "Let's go to Disneyland tonight and just ride Space Mountain," or, "Anyone want churros? Let's go to Disneyland and have some churros." I look back on that childhood and pinch myself to remember those moments—that privilege I had often taken for granted, as would any kid who didn't know differently. (Sorry to my own kids that they had to grow up far away from any Disney location.)

The Disney bug didn't leave me when I left California, though. I participated in two Disney internships as a college student and was able to work at Disney's Animal Kingdom and Disney's Old Key West Resort. I thought being a kid at Disney couldn't be beat, but turns out, being an adult at Disney is even better!

Of course, life gets busier every year, and as much as I'd love to, taking a trip to California or Florida every few months just isn't feasible for me now. And it really isn't for the average family either. Several years ago, I decided to do something about it by re-creating that magic at home. I started making Disney Park–inspired foods and snacks from scratch, and before long, friends started to request I make them for group gatherings. My blog posts about Disney recipes became popular, and my kids were always begging me to make them "The Grey Stuff." That's when I realized that Disney fans need this book, and I'm just the person to write it for them.

So whether you are new to the Disney fandom or you have been a Disney devotee all your life, you can finally enjoy Disney Park snacks and treats any day of the year. Wow your friends at your next Disney movie viewing party with French Fries with Pulled Pork and Cheese. Delight your children with a Chocolate-Hazelnut Lunch Box Tart. Add Cheeseburger Steamed Pods to your regular dinner menu. However you use these recipes, you'll discover deliciousness on each page. I'm excited for you to try them in your own kitchen!

Introduction

Dole Whip at Magic Kingdom, Mickey Pretzels at Disney's Hollywood Studios, Frozen Lemonade at Disney's Animal Kingdom—Disney has so much to offer, and one of its best attractions is its food! Of course, a trip to Disney isn't always in the cards, but luckily you can bring its treats straight to your own kitchen.

The Unofficial Disney Parks Cookbook offers one hundred easy recipes for the best of Disney's magical cuisine. Whether you've been to the parks a hundred times and are craving your favorite Disney dishes, or you're just looking for something Disney-inspired to make you feel like you're on vacation, each recipe has been thoroughly tested to ensure a taste worthy of a certain mouse. The recipes are also organized based on the Disney Park where each one is featured, beginning with the first park to open, Disneyland, and ending with the newest park, Disney California Adventure. You'll find treats for every occasion, including:

- Disneyland's nostalgic delights, like Beignets and Jungle Juleps

- Disney's Hollywood Studios' best snacks to kick off any Disney marathon, from Perfect Popcorn to Candy Apples

- EPCOT's international fare, like honey-drenched Moroccan Baklava and French Napoleons

- Disney California Adventure go-tos for an at-home island retreat, from Mangonada Smoothies to Chili-Lime Corn on the Cob

- Magic Kingdom's fairytale favorites, like Peter Pan Floats and Gaston's Giant Cinnamon Rolls

Flip through to recipes you know and love or try something new! Just one bite and you may be transported to Neverland to become a kid again. Or perhaps you will find yourself in a galaxy far, far away.

Wherever your taste buds lead, the magic of Disney will glow within your kitchen. But before you grab an apron—and maybe your favorite mouse ears too—be sure to check out Part 1 for more information on each Disney Park and the foods found there, as well as tools you will want to have on hand to create the recipes in this book. With these basics, you'll be ready to get cooking!

PART 1

DISNEY PARKS COOKING 101

Disney is well known for being a titan of the food industry. Over the years, what began as a single theme park in California grew into a twelve-park empire across three continents. Creating satisfying cuisine for the millions of visitors they welcome not only takes an army of Cast Members, but mountains of food and industrial supplies. Luckily for you, *The Unofficial Disney Parks Cookbook* has re-envisioned one hundred of these recipes with a home kitchen in mind!

In this part, you'll explore the food and beverages of Disney's six main US parks in more detail, from the classics introduced by Walt Disney himself at Disneyland to modern favorites created for the newer attractions at Disney California Adventure. Chapter 1 sets the stage for the recipes included in Part 2, cluing you in to the different food themes and specific meals, treats, and drinks you'll find in each park chapter. Then, before tying on that apron, you'll want to check out the chapter on essential tools. Here, you'll discover everything you will need for creating tasty Disney dishes right in your own kitchen. Let the magic begin!

CHAPTER 1

The Delicious Disney Experience

The Disney Parks at both Disneyland and Walt Disney World have so much to offer, and food is an important part of the experience. Not only do you need to stay energized through full days of park attractions, but there are also countless mouthwatering recipes you will only find at these parks. In this chapter, you'll explore the snacks and treats offered at each US Disney Park, from classics such as Churros and Mickey Pretzels to newer favorites like Peter Pan Floats and frozen Night Blossoms. This chapter, and the recipes that follow in Part 2, serve to magnify your enjoyment of Disney, both in the different parks and at home. Let's dive in—there's so much magic to uncover!

Disneyland

On July 17, 1955, crowds came from everywhere to see if the experiment by film mogul Walt Disney was going to sink or swim. Construction crews worked around the clock to get everything ready for opening morning, but it got so tight that Walt Disney had to decide whether plumbers should finish the toilets or the drinking fountains, since they only had time to complete one. He chose the toilets, and that choice demonstrated that Walt Disney was concentrating on food sales as much as he was the rides. After all, without working drinking fountains, everyone would turn to the park offerings to quench their thirst.

The Long Beach Independent Telegram ran an ad in July 1955 that talked up the food options for the new Disneyland:

Good Eating Land at Disneyland!
Like Adventureland and Fantasyland, the new
"Kingdom of Good Eating" at Disneyland is another
great attraction. Fine restaurants, unique refreshment
stands and interesting luncheon spots abound in
Disneyland. Dining Disneyland style
is an unforgettable experience. The food's
as fabulous as the fun, too!

Sponsored foods included the Chicken of the Sea Pirate Ship and Restaurant. Forty-three well-known brands contracted with Disneyland to serve food and to serve it Walt's way, with elaborate theming. Walt knew food could be more than just sustenance. The idea seems obvious today, but in post–Depression America, food was not usually especially flavorful or frivolous. People ate what they needed to survive, and that was about it. Snacks and treats, especially, were a relatively new concept.

Disneyland began with treats that were new and fun in the 1950s and continues to serve them to this day, not for the novelty that they used to be, but for the nostalgia. Foods like cotton candy, popcorn, turkey legs, and funnel cakes transport us back to images of a simpler time.

Today's Disneyland food culture has taken on an even bigger persona—one that has adapted over time. Some food items, like Dole Whip, have become cult classics and draw extremely long lines and massive online hashtag followings. "Social Clubs" have popped up in the parks: exclusive groups that have catchy names (like "Neverlanders" and "Main Street Elite") and personalized jackets. Many of these groups' identities revolve around food items offered at Disneyland. While the look of the food may have changed in many ways, Disneyland is and always will be a place where families go to have fun and enjoy food favorites.

Magic Kingdom

Although Disneyland and the Magic Kingdom are "twin" parks, they do have several distinct differences. Magic Kingdom's biggest food advantage over Disneyland is its ability to produce massive volumes of fare for the huge crowds it gets every day. Cosmic Ray's Starlight Café, a quick-service restaurant located in Magic Kingdom's Tomorrowland, is Disney Parks' busiest restaurant—the busiest restaurant in the United States, in fact, and the third busiest in the world. Not Disney World—the whole world. Walt Disney World takes in about 52 million visitors annually, and all those people need to be fed!

Just as Disneyland began by contracting out food production to other companies, Magic Kingdom continued this tradition. Although the food items often don't broadcast the companies that make them anymore, most snacks and treats sold at Disney Parks are created in factories, and often by third-party companies. This ensures supply to match the massive demand and gives guests the highest quality product on the market, as well as uniform quality.

In order to bring that food to the masses at Magic Kingdom, The Walt Disney Company also built a system of tunnels underground. These Utilidors are on the "first floor" of Florida (due to the high water table), while the streets of the park are located on the "second floor." These efficient tunnels allow fresh food and drink to be whisked straight to the restaurants, and in turn, food waste to be removed from the park.

Another efficient invention of the Magic Kingdom is the Disney College Program. This internship program, started in 1972 (just one year after Magic Kingdom opened), supplies the necessary workforce to serve those millions of guests. College students from around the country and around the world come out in droves to be a part of the magic. They are the primary employees of all food establishments at the Magic Kingdom, including food carts and counter and table service restaurants. If a university is listed as an employee's "hometown" on their Disney nametag, this is an indication that they are a Disney College Program participant!

Magic Kingdom is now a well-oiled machine and rarely encounters hiccups in an operating day. These carefully planned actions guarantee hungry guests are made happy.

EPCOT

Disney's real leap of faith came in 1982, with the opening of EPCOT at Walt Disney World. Instead of a hub-and-spoke setup, this park was divided into two sections: Future World and the World Showcase. Disney soon realized that EPCOT's World Showcase would become a culinary mecca. Where else in the world can you get authentic cuisine from eleven different countries all in one day? Most countries have at least one flagship table service restaurant to show off the finest food, along with several counter service and grab-and-go snack and treat options.

One popular way to experience EPCOT is to "drink around the world," enjoying an alcoholic beverage in each of the eleven countries. A growing trend is also to "snack around the world," or try at least one snack or treat from each country. This gives guests an opportunity to take in the country not only with their eyes but also with their taste buds!

EPCOT hosts several festivals every year, including the EPCOT International Food and Wine Festival. Guests travel around the park and sample small bites and wine varieties from booths representing countries in the World Showcase, as well as some countries other than those permanently represented at EPCOT. Disney has made it even easier for guests to buy food at this festival by instituting a Food and Wine Passport, where guests prepay for a punch-style card that lists different food items to pick up. Sometimes favorites from the Food and Wine Festival also become new menu items at different spots around Walt Disney World. Celebrity chefs don aprons and dazzle audiences with cooking demonstrations at the American Gardens Theatre, and popular food companies come to present their products.

Even the other EPCOT festivals, like the International Flower and Garden Festival and the International Festival of the Arts, include a food focus. Interactive treats like paintable cookies are fun for kids and adults alike. People may come for the flowers or art, but they certainly stay for the unique food offerings available.

EPCOT also has a dedication to sustainability in food production. Disney-goers can even see it firsthand on the ride Living with the Land, which takes guests on a boat ride through innovative greenhouses that produce foods used in Walt Disney World kitchens. Cutting-edge technologies, like hydroponics and sand gardening, are used in these greenhouses. And the Behind the Seeds tour treats guests to an in-depth look at Disney's commitment to less food waste and more productive farming methods.

Disney's Hollywood Studios

Disney's Hollywood Studios is the most eclectic of the Disney Parks, its unifying theme being "stories inspired by movies"—which can be just about anything! Because of that, its food culture is also across the board, from extremely fine dining at The Hollywood Brown Derby to common comfort foods at Woody's Lunch Box. But no matter the theme, Disney's Hollywood Studios has been bringing the flavor since 1989.

Inspired by the golden age of Hollywood, guests become immersed in glitz and glamor the moment they walk through the gates. Stroll down Hollywood Boulevard to The Trolley Car Café for some morning coffee or tea and a gigantic Butterfinger Cupcake (see recipe in Chapter 6)!

While there have always been snacks and treat options available at Disney's Hollywood Studios, the park has historically weighed more heavily on table service meals. With six restaurants in the park, designers planned for guests to take time out of their day to sit for an hour or two and enjoy a slow meal.

The landscape of Disney's Hollywood Studios drastically changed between 2018 and 2019, when two new areas opened in quick succession—Toy Story Land and Star Wars: Galaxy's Edge. These new lands would redefine the park's culinary identity and provide new and exciting snacks and treats for guests.

Toy Story Land opened in 2018 and brought three major attractions and one counter service dining location. Woody's Lunch Box quickly rose in the ranks to become one of the most popular eateries in the park. Offering quick and filling classic American comfort food like Pop-Tarts–style snacks and grilled cheese and barbecue sandwiches, this location has consistently long lines of guests waiting to get their hands on some grub.

Star Wars: Galaxy's Edge opened in the fall of 2019. Oga's Cantina created a brand-new category of dining never before seen at Disney— a family-friendly bar! At Oga's, both adults and children are accepted, with Cast Members serving both alcoholic (to guests aged twenty-one and up, of course) and non-alcoholic signature drinks.

And for anyone not wanting to wait for a seat at the bar, the Milk Stand is available to quench your thirst with Blue and Green Milks. Other quick-service meals and snack locations include Docking Bay 7 Food and Cargo, Ronto Roasters, and Kat Saka's Kettle. Each has inventive alien fare perfect for a quick bite on the way from one attraction to another.

Interestingly, Toy Story Land and Star Wars: Galaxy's Edge both opened with no table service restaurants, a direct change from the previous feel of the park. Instead of encouraging guests to take time to slow down and eat a meal, now the aim seems to be to keep guests moving and riding and seeing! The perfect marriage of delicious food and quick convenience is a hit with guests.

Disney's Animal Kingdom

There are two things that make Disney's Animal Kingdom stand out from the other parks: live animals and immersive storytelling. It has always been first and foremost an authentic cultural experience. Imagineer Joe Rohde conceived of the whole park and did extensive research in Africa and Asia to design lands that truly transport the guests straight into the heart of these continents.

The food is also an immersive experience. For example, outside the roller coaster Expedition Everest—Legend of the Forbidden Mountain is an ice cream truck. But the truck has a broken axle on the front with the wheel smashed in. Legend has it that the owner of the truck used to drive all over "Serka Zong" selling his ice cream, but one day the truck broke down. The owner planned to get the truck fixed, but patrons just started to line up at the truck, so he thought, "What the heck! I'll just sell here permanently." And if you talk to

Cast Members working at any snack stand, restaurant, or attraction and ask them the backstory of their place of work, they can regale you with a fictitious tale that sounds true!

Pandora—The World of Avatar (situated to the left of Animal Kingdom's entrance and opened to the public in 2017) presented a unique challenge to Imagineers: How could they create delicious food that seemed genuinely alien? In order to produce this effect, they played with textures and colors. The popular Night Blossoms drink has jelly boba balls inside that have a silly, slippery feel in your mouth; the Blueberry Cream Cheese Mousse is a playful dome shape not usually seen in cheesecakes (see both recipes in Chapter 7). In Animal Kingdom, delicious treats and amazing storytelling experiences greet you around every bend.

Disney California Adventure

Decades after Disneyland first opened, Disney finally opened a "second gate" in California in 2001. Rather than focusing on Americana in general, Disney California Adventure shines a light on the culture of the Golden State.

From one end of the park to the other, Mexican roots within California are felt and tasted—from Studio Catering Co.'s Backlot Nachos all the way to Paradise Garden Grill's Carnitas Tacos and Cocina Cucamonga Mexican Grill in Pacific Wharf. The annual Food and Wine Festival at California Adventure also prominently features Mexican dishes. Disney wanted to show the Mexican connection to the state as well as cater to the Hispanic guests who make up a huge percentage of visitors.

Another group widely celebrated in the park are the people of Asia. Lucky Fortune Cookery serves up delicious Pan-Asian cuisine representing Beijing, Seoul, Bangkok, and Tokyo. Disney California Adventure also holds a Lunar New Year festival each year, with special food and merchandise booths available only during the festival.

Northern California certainly leads the state in wine, and this park capitalizes on that. From Sonoma Terrace to Alfresco Tasting Terrace, California wines flow for the adult population at the park. Boudin Bakery, the most popular sourdough bread producer in the country, is featured in a factory tour attraction and through sourdough menu items at Pacific Wharf Café.

Once the park started to shift in 2007 from focusing on California themes to Disney's lucrative intellectual properties, like Pixar and Marvel, it began re-creating favorite snacks and treats shown on screen. It was a big hit. Who wouldn't want to try Jack-Jack's Num Num Cookies that he eats in *Incredibles 2* (see recipe in Chapter 8)? Or have cotton candy like Bing Bong from *Inside Out*? Flo's V8 Café in Cars Land is an exact replica of the one in the film franchise—you are transported right to her café!

The blend of authentic cuisines and inventive movie offerings has made Disney California Adventure a park worthy of great food lovers.

Your Disney Cuisine

Whether you visit Disney Parks every year, you've been once or twice before, or you're still planning that first magical trip, this book was created to help you transform your own kitchen into a world Walt Disney himself would be proud of. You will soon be making amazing snacks, meals, desserts, and more like the pros—just be sure to check out the next chapter on kitchen essentials before pulling out that chef's hat!

CHAPTER 2

The Disney Cook's Essentials

What is a cook without their tools? Before jumping into the recipes in the next part, you'll want to ensure your kitchen is fully stocked with the essentials for creating the following recipes. In this chapter, you'll explore everything you need to whip up each delicious dish in Part 2. The different tools are listed in alphabetical order, so you can easily flip back to a certain item at any time. You're well on your way to stirring up some Disney magic in your own home!

Baking Sheets

Baking sheets come in many shapes and sizes, but the best ones for the recipes in this book have ½"-tall sides and are called "half sheets."

Blender

A good-quality, high-power stand blender will help you achieve a smoother consistency for smoothies and dips. Start with a low setting and turn up the speed as larger pieces break up.

Cake Pans

Standard 9" cake pans will help you create soft, flavorful sponges, as in the Bavarian Cheesecake recipe. Typically you line these pans with parchment paper to prevent sticking.

Cookie Cutters

Owning a set of Mickey cookie cutters should be a priority for any Disney chef, but if you aren't there in your culinary journey yet, have no fear. A makeshift Mickey cutter can be made in one of two ways. In the first way, trace a Mickey shape (one larger circle with two smaller circles positioned as ears) on a piece of paper and trace this drawing with your knife in your dough. Alternatively, use one large cup and two smaller cups to press the Mickey shape into the dough before cutting.

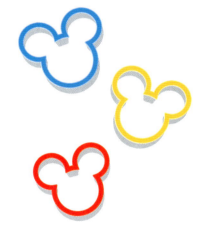

Cookie Scoop

Cookie scoops help make uniform half-ball shapes. They look like ice cream scoops and have a half-circle top and a spring-squeeze handle. The smallest scoops are about 1 tablespoon, medium scoops about 2½ tablespoons, and large scoops about 4 tablespoons.

Cooling Rack

A common wire cooling/drying rack is sufficient for the recipes in this book. They are typically made from stainless steel and have straight lines or a crosshatch pattern.

Electric Pressure Cooker

Many different brands are available, but any dependable electric pressure cooker will do. Make sure that there is a properly sized inner pot placed in the cooker, and that you are careful to avoid steam burns when you release pressure. Electric pressure cookers can save a lot of time in the kitchen and provide a delicious product.

Food Coloring

Many of the following recipes use food coloring to pull off the original Disney look. Gel colors are always preferred, as they have a brighter pop of color than liquid food coloring, and the tighter consistency won't change the texture of the dish. If your gel colors come in pots and cannot "drop," use a wooden toothpick to dip into the gel and swipe it through the food you want to color. Repeat with each drop needed.

Food Processor

Food processors are basically high-powered blenders that specialize in chopping dry foods. If you don't have a food processor, a blender works about as well. If you have neither, chopping with a knife very finely works too—it is just more labor-intensive and less uniform.

Grill or Grill Pan

For items that need to be grilled, an outdoor grill and indoor grill pan are interchangeable. Propane grills should be preheated to ensure even cooking. Indoor grill pans need to be greased with cooking oil before using to help prevent sticking. Charcoal grills can also be used; they just require more prep and cleanup. Consult your grill instructions for safe cooking guidelines.

Ice Cream Machine

The easiest ice cream machines are the ones with a freezable "bowl." This bowl is removed from the freezer moments before use, and ice cream or drink mix is poured directly into the frozen bowl. The bowl then spins on a base and a paddle mixes and scrapes the inside. Other options are available if you are unable to use this type of ice cream machine. For example, you can use an ice cream bucket-type machine that requires ice cubes and rock salt. Just pour the mixture from the recipe into the metal inner-container and fill the outer bucket with ice and rock salt. Run the machine until the consistency matches the recipe description. Any machine you have is fine; some are just more hassle than others.

Immersion Blender

Immersion blenders are convenient because you can leave your soup or sauce in the pot on the stove and purée it without moving to a stand blender or food processor. If you don't have one, however, these other options work just as well.

Muffin Pans

Several recipes in this book require muffin or cupcake pans. Standard muffin pans typically have twelve cups, mini-muffin pans have twenty-four small cups, and jumbo muffin pans have six large cups.

Paper Grocery Bags

All flavored popcorn recipes in this book use large paper grocery bags to mix the topping with the popcorn. This is a method that ensures an even coating and flavor distribution. If you do not have access to large paper grocery bags, you can simply toss the seasonings and popcorn together in an extra-large bowl.

Parchment Paper

Almost every recipe in this book that requires baking will instruct you to line your baking sheet or pan with parchment paper. This simple step ensures a more even baking surface, more consistent browning, and greatly reduces the likelihood of your food sticking to the pan. Parchment paper can be found in any grocery store.

Piping Bags

Many recipes in this book call for piping bags, but you don't have to own a fancy set. A heavy-duty plastic sandwich or gallon bag will do nicely. Simply load the dough or other mixture into the bag, then snip a small edge off one of the bottom corners. Start your hole out small and make it bigger as needed.

PIPING BAG TIPS

Some recipes will call for special piping bag tips, such as a large star tip for Churros (see recipe in Chapter 3). While you don't need to use a tip for any recipe that follows, it can make for an eye-catching design. Churros especially benefit from a star tip because the deep grooves create that signature crunch, and the grooves help the cinnamon and sugar to adhere.

Popsicle Molds

Plastic Popsicle molds are inexpensive and can be found in most grocery or big-box stores. However, if you don't have one, you can use small plastic or paper cups instead. Simply pour in your Popsicle mix and cover the cup with aluminum foil. Push a Popsicle stick through the foil in the center of the cup. The foil will stabilize the stick and keep it in the center.

Popsicle Sticks

Wooden Popsicle sticks can be bought in bulk online or at most grocery stores. Popsicle molds will have built-in slots for the sticks to be inserted.

Pots and Pans

Heavy-bottomed saucepans are preferred in many recipes. The thick metal bottom regulates the temperature better and prevents burning. If you don't have heavy-bottomed pans, any appropriately sized pot or pan will do; just keep an extra close eye on foods cooking on the stove. Stir more frequently to prevent burning.

Ramekins

Ramekin is just a fancy word for a small glass or ceramic bowl that can be baked in the oven. Jack-Jack's Num Num Cookies (see recipe in Chapter 8) and Baked Lobster Macaroni & Cheese (see recipe in Chapter 7) call for these bowls. If you don't have designated ramekins, check the bottom of your glass storage containers or cereal bowls to see if they are oven safe.

Rolling Pin

Rolling pins come in many shapes and sizes, including those that have handles on the sides, French styles, and the straight cylindrical style. Any variety is fine for use in the following recipes.

Shaved Ice Maker

The Kakigōri recipes in this book (see recipes in Chapter 5) call for a shaved ice maker. These range from multi-thousand-dollar machines that expertly shave the ice using a razor-thin blade to cheap models found in most grocery or big-box stores. Any machine you have is fine. It is difficult to shave ice without a specialized machine; however, some high-end blenders have the capability to crush ice finely enough to use in these recipes.

Sieve/Sifter

The sifters and sieves described in the following recipes refer to a stainless steel mesh half-dome strainer. Get one with a medium-fine mesh.

Springform Pan

A standard 9" springform pan has a removable bottom in the shape of a circle and sides that clinch together with a clip. This kind of pan is essential so a cheesecake removes easily after setting.

Stand Mixer

Almost any recipe in this book that requires mixing uses a stand mixer. This machine makes mixing, whipping, and kneading easy and uniform. If you don't have a stand mixer, the second-best option is a hand mixer. These often also have interchangeable attachments for mixing or whipping. If you have neither, of course you can mix, whip, and knead by hand—it will just take a bit more strength and stamina.

Steamer Basket

For the Cheeseburger Steamed Pods (see recipe in Chapter 7) in this book, a steamer basket is used. This is a metal or bamboo basket that has holes in the bottom and sits atop a pot of boiling water and utilizes steam to gently cook the food. A rice cooker with a steamer basket can be used instead of the stovetop version.

Thermometers

A confection or candy thermometer is essential for any candy making or deep-frying. Bringing mixtures to the correct temperature changes the way the final product's texture and taste will turn out. A meat thermometer is crucial when assuring that meat is cooked to a safe temperature. Both types of thermometers can be bought at most grocery and big-box stores.

Wooden Skewers

For skewer recipes, 8" wooden skewers are recommended. Be sure to soak them in water prior to use so they don't burn up on the grill. Longer, shorter, or metal skewers are all fine to use as well if you don't have the recommended wooden skewers.

Getting Started

Now that you've explored the main tools you'll want to have on hand, you are ready to get cooking! Remember: Although these recipes are modeled after Disney Park originals, the food you create is unique to you. Experiment with whatever flavors and designs your heart desires and have fun with it. When in doubt, refer back to the kitchen essentials. It's time to whip up some delicious magic!

PART 2

MAGICAL RECIPES

Welcome to the (quite literal) meat and potatoes of Disney Parks! That's right, Part 2 is all about the recipes. In the following chapters, you will find one hundred delicious snacks, meals, desserts, and drinks inspired by the classic and modern favorites at Disney's six US parks. Check out the map at the beginning of each chapter to see where each food item is (or was originally) served at the park.

The chapters in this part are organized by the date each park opened, beginning with Walt Disney's pioneer attraction, Disneyland, and ending with the 2001 Disney California Adventure. While at the Magic Kingdom, stop on Main Street for a Cookies and Cream Cupcake, or chart your course for a Sweet-and-Spicy Chicken Waffle Sandwich in Liberty Square. Perhaps you've got your eye on a Star Wars adventure courtesy of Disney's Hollywood Studios, sipping on Blue Milk between battles. Or maybe it's a trip through beloved Pixar films you desire: Just be sure to treat yourself to a Pixar Pier Frosty Parfait. Your kitchen is just moments away from being magically transported to Disney—no actual travel required!

CHAPTER 3

Disneyland

Nothing quite compares to your first Disneyland trip. No matter what age you were, or if it has yet to come, it is a magical day that will remain pixie-dusted in your memory. After you scan your ticket at the front gate, you walk onto Main Street, U.S.A. At the end of Main Street is a hub featuring the iconic Sleeping Beauty Castle. From there, you can branch out to the different "lands": Adventureland, Frontierland, Critter Country, New Orleans Square, Star Wars: Galaxy's Edge, Mickey's Toontown, Fantasyland, and Tomorrowland. Food options at Disneyland tend to highlight each land's theme, from the bayou fixings in New Orleans Square to colorful confections at Maurice's Treats in Fantasyland. As unique as each land's foods are, however, there is a unifying theme to Disneyland's snack culture—a carefree trip to midcentury America. Walt Disney wanted families to have yummy snacks easily available at every turn in Disneyland. In this chapter, you'll discover recipes for fan favorites in each of Disneyland's unique lands.

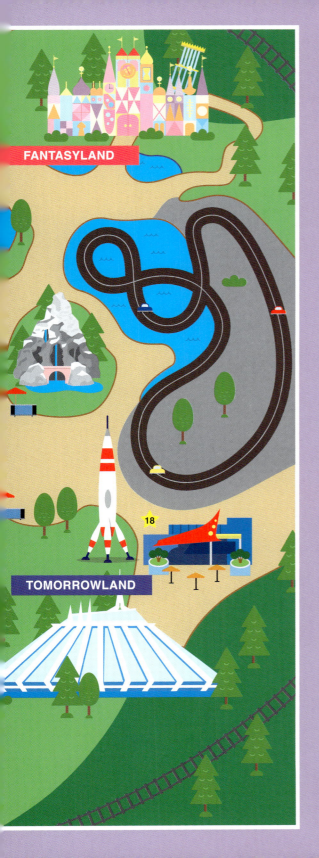

★ 1 **CHURROS** (Main Street, U.S.A., Disneyland)

★ 2 **RASPBERRY ROSE MICKEY MACARONS** (Main Street, U.S.A., Disneyland)

★ 3 **COOKIES AND CREAM MICKEY CUPCAKES** (Main Street, U.S.A., Disneyland)

★ 4 **BENGAL BEEF SKEWERS** (Adventureland, Disneyland)

★ 5 **JUNGLE JULEPS** (Adventureland, Disneyland)

★ 6 **TIGER TAIL BREADSTICKS** (Adventureland, Disneyland)

★ 7 **HUMMUS TRIO** (Adventureland, Disneyland)

★ 8 **PORK BELLY SKEWERS** (Adventureland, Disneyland)

★ 9 **SAFARI SKEWERS** (Adventureland, Disneyland)

★ 10 **BEIGNETS** (New Orleans Square, Disneyland)

★ 11 **FRITTERS** (New Orleans Square, Disneyland)

★ 12 **CLAM CHOWDER** (New Orleans Square, Disneyland)

★ 13 **MINT JULEPS** (New Orleans Square, Disneyland)

★ 14 **GOLD PORT GALLEY LEMONADE** (Critter Country, Disneyland)

★ 15 **CHURRO FUNNEL CAKE** (Critter Country, Disneyland)

★ 16 **THE GREY STUFF GÂTEAU** (Fantasyland, Disneyland)

★ 17 **MATTERHORN MACAROONS** (Fantasyland, Disneyland)

★ 18 **BROWNIE BITES** (Tomorrowland, Disneyland)

Churros

Main Street, U.S.A., Disneyland

· · · · ✦ · · · ·

According to www.popsugar.com, 2.8 million churros are sold at Disneyland every year. That's a lot of dough! Churros are among the most constant and versatile foods sold at Disney Parks. This classic version can be found at food carts near Sleeping Beauty Castle. Try pairing your own with some chocolate dipping sauce for a rich treat.

YIELDS 6 CHURROS

1 cup room-temperature water

3 tablespoons plus ½ cup granulated sugar, divided

½ teaspoon salt

3 tablespoons plus 4 cups vegetable oil, divided

1 cup all-purpose flour

1 teaspoon ground cinnamon

1. Line an ungreased baking sheet with parchment paper and set aside.

2. In a large saucepan over medium-high heat, add water, 3 tablespoons sugar, salt, and 3 tablespoons oil. Stir until mixture reaches a boil, about 4 minutes, then remove from heat.

3. Add flour and stir until combined.

4. Scoop dough into a large piping bag fitted with a large star tip. Let dough cool until you are able to hold the bag comfortably, about 10 minutes.

5. Pipe dough into 6" lines onto prepared baking sheet. Place sheet into freezer to set 1 hour.

6. In a large, heavy-bottomed pot over medium-high heat, add remaining 4 cups oil. It should measure to a depth of about 3". Heat until oil reaches 375°F. Line a large plate with paper towels and set aside.

7. In a medium shallow bowl, combine remaining sugar and cinnamon. Set aside.

8. Carefully slide one Churro into hot oil. Flip while frying until golden brown, about 2 minutes total.

9. Remove from oil with tongs and place in bowl with sugar-cinnamon mixture. Turn to coat Churro thoroughly, and transfer to lined plate to cool. Repeat with remaining Churros.

Raspberry Rose Mickey Macarons

Main Street, U.S.A., Disneyland

· · · · ✦ · · · ·

The Jolly Holiday Bakery Café has only been on Disneyland's Main Street, U.S.A., since 2012. Prior to that, the location was the home of the Blue Ribbon Bakery. Before 1990, it was the Sunkist Citrus House. A lot of changes have occurred on Main Street, U.S.A., over the years, but it always maintains a classic, nostalgic feel—an ambiance that is perfectly captured in the café's Raspberry Rose Mickey Macarons. These delicious, eye-catching pink macarons were introduced in 2014 and have been a mainstay of the Jolly Holiday Bakery Café ever since. For added flair, decorate the top of each macaron with a stripe of edible gold paint.

YIELDS 6 LARGE MACARONS

For Raspberry Mousse

1 (¼-ounce) packet
  unflavored gelatin
½ cup cold water, divided
12 ounces fresh raspberries
⅔ cup granulated sugar
1½ cups heavy cream

1. In a medium bowl, empty gelatin pack into ¼ cup cold water. Set aside.

2. In a medium saucepan over medium heat, add 12 ounces raspberries, sugar, and remaining ¼ cup water. Heat until hot and bubbly, about 5 minutes, then mash mixture with a spoon.

3. Pour mixture into a blender, cover, and purée. Using a fine-mesh strainer, strain purée back into saucepan over medium heat.

4. Add gelatin mix and heat until it comes to a boil, about 4 minutes. Boil 1 minute, stirring constantly.

5. Remove pot from heat and allow to cool to room temperature, about 15 minutes.

(continued) ▶

6. In bowl of a stand mixer, use the whisk attachment to whip heavy cream on high speed until stiff peaks form, about 4 minutes. Add cooled berry mix and fold in with a spatula until completely combined.

7. Transfer to a medium container, cover, and refrigerate until ready to add to Macarons, at least 1 hour.

For Macaron Shells

- 3 large egg whites, at room temperature
- ¼ teaspoon cream of tartar
- ¼ cup granulated sugar
- 1 cup almond flour
- 1½ cups confectioners' sugar
- 5 drops dark pink gel food coloring
- 12 medium fresh raspberries

1. Line a large ungreased baking sheet with parchment paper and set aside.

2. In the clean bowl of a stand mixer, add egg whites. Using the whisk attachment, whip whites on high speed 1 minute, then add cream of tartar. Whip another minute, then add granulated sugar and whip until stiff peaks form, about 4 minutes. Set aside.

3. Into a medium bowl, sift almond flour and confectioners' sugar. Stir to combine. Pour half the mixture into whipped egg whites and carefully fold in with a spatula. Add remaining flour mixture to egg whites and fold until just combined. Fold in food coloring.

4. Add mixture to a large piping bag. Cut the tip off the bottom or fit with a round tip. Squeeze three disks (one 1½" and two 1") of Macaron mixture onto prepared baking sheet to form a Mickey face. Repeat piping until baking sheet is filled or batter is used up.

5. Firmly tap the baking sheet against a table or countertop about ten times to settle the batter and knock out any bubbles. Let sit at room temperature 45 minutes.

6. Preheat oven to 300°F. Bake shells 18 minutes, or until macarons are barely brown around the outside.

7. Remove from oven and let cool on baking sheet completely, about 20 minutes. Once cooled, move Macaron Shells from sheet onto a cutting board and flip over half of the Macaron Shells. On the back of each flipped shell, place a dollop of mousse followed by a raspberry (alternating mousse and raspberries) until back of shell is covered. Sandwich with remaining Macaron Shells.

Cookies and Cream Mickey Cupcakes

Main Street, U.S.A., Disneyland

· · · · ✦ · · · ·

Candy Palace on Main Street, U.S.A., was renovated in 2012 and given a very sweet interior. Many of the features are meant to look edible, such as the chandelier that seems to be dripping ice cream, and the exit sign shaped as a wrapped candy. And among its actually edible creations are delectable, supersweet Cookies and Cream Mickey Cupcakes. Topped with the iconic mouse ears, these popular treats are easy to whip up and sure to please.

YIELDS 24 CUPCAKES

For Cupcakes

3 tablespoons salted butter, softened
1½ cups granulated sugar
2 large eggs
1 teaspoon vanilla extract
1⅓ cups all-purpose flour
¼ teaspoon baking soda
2 teaspoons baking powder
¾ cup cocoa powder
¼ teaspoon salt
1 cup whole milk

1. Preheat oven to 350°F. Line two standard muffin tins with cupcake liners and set aside.

2. In the bowl of a stand mixer, add butter and sugar. Using the flat beater attachment, cream together well. Add eggs and vanilla. While mixer is running, add flour, baking soda, baking powder, cocoa powder, and salt; continue mixing until well combined. Add milk slowly.

3. Scoop batter into prepared muffin tins, filling cups just above halfway.

4. Bake 15 minutes or until a toothpick inserted in the middle comes out clean. Remove from oven and allow to cool completely, about 1 hour, before frosting.

(continued) ▶

For Frosting

½ cup salted butter, softened

4 cups confectioners' sugar

8 ounces cream cheese, softened

2 tablespoons heavy cream

10 chocolate sandwich cookies, crushed

48 mini chocolate sandwich cookies, whole

1. In the clean bowl of a stand mixer, add butter, confectioners' sugar, cream cheese, and heavy cream. Using the flat beater attachment, whip until light and fluffy. Add crushed cookies and mix until combined.

2. Scoop Frosting into a piping bag fitted with a large star tip. Swirl a generous amount of Frosting on each Cupcake, creating a pointed mound. Stand a mini sandwich cookie upright on either side of pointed mound to create Mickey Mouse ears.

MIX IT UP

Frosting swirls are adorable, but if you prefer less frosting on your cupcakes, you can just use a knife to spread a thinner layer of frosting on top of the cupcakes—enough to push in the mouse ears.

Bengal Beef Skewers

Adventureland, Disneyland

· · · · ✦ · · ·

Tucked right across the way from Indiana Jones Adventure is Bengal Barbecue, a jungle-themed kiosk best known for its skewers and open view of the Cast Members working at the grill. Open for over twenty-five years, this snack spot (and the ferocious tiger out front!) has become an iconic stop for anyone visiting Adventureland. Missing the Jungle Cruise? Want some Indiana Jones–inspired action? Try this hearty barbecue recipe! Serve with a fresh garden salad for a health boost.

SERVES 6

½ cup teriyaki sauce
½ cup soy sauce
⅓ cup rice vinegar
1 tablespoon red wine vinegar
½ teaspoon garlic powder
1 tablespoon minced fresh ginger
¾ cup light brown sugar
3 tablespoons cold water
3 tablespoons cornstarch
1 (1-pound) package kebab beef
6 (8") wooden skewers

1. In a medium saucepan over medium heat, add teriyaki sauce, soy sauce, rice vinegar, red wine vinegar, garlic powder, ginger, and brown sugar. Bring to a boil, stirring often.

2. In a small bowl, mix water and cornstarch together.

3. Once sauce comes to a boil, remove from heat and gradually stir in cornstarch mixture. Allow sauce to cool, about 20 minutes. Pour half the sauce into a shallow dish.

4. Add meat chunks to shallow dish and stir to coat. Refrigerate covered overnight to marinate. Refrigerate remaining sauce in a separate covered container.

5. When ready to assemble skewers, soak wooden skewers in water 30 minutes. Thread saucy meat chunks onto skewers.

6. Preheat grill or grill pan 10 minutes to medium heat.

7. Dip a folded paper towel in olive oil and hold with tongs to grease the grill. Lay skewers on grill and spread reserved sauce generously over meat while it cooks. Grill 8 minutes or until preferred doneness, flipping meat skewers a few times during cooking.

Jungle Juleps

Adventureland, Disneyland

· · · ✦ · · ·

Indiana Jones Adventure may be classified as a "thrill ride," but actually, it hits a top speed of only 14 miles per hour—barely neighborhood driving speeds. Imagineers were able to create the effect of speed and danger by programming the onboard computers to deliver a curated experience using hydraulics. This drink mimics the "punch" of the ride—all the flavor and excitement, with no alcohol! You can also get creative with this drink. Instead of orange or grape juice, try passion fruit, mango, or pineapple, for example.

SERVES 2

2 cups frozen pineapple chunks
1 cup pulp-free orange juice
1 cup 100% grape juice
¼ cup lemon juice
2 tablespoons granulated sugar

Add all ingredients to a blender and blend until smooth.

Tiger Tail Breadsticks

Adventureland, Disneyland

. . . . ✦ . . . .

Tiger Tail Breadsticks are delicious on their own, but a fun way to enjoy this snack is to dip them in hummus from the Hummus Trio dish in this chapter. You can also make the other Bengal Barbecue recipes included in this book and serve them on a charcuterie-style board. Don't forget the Jungle Juleps (see recipe in this chapter) on the side too! Tiger Tail Breadsticks act as a perfect carb to cleanse the palate.

SERVES 8

¼ cup plus 1 cup warm water (110°F), divided
½ teaspoon plus 1 tablespoon granulated sugar, divided
1 (¼-ounce) packet active dry yeast
4 cups all-purpose flour, divided
½ teaspoon salt
1 tablespoon salted butter, melted
1 teaspoon minced garlic
1 cup shredded Cheddar cheese

1. Pour ¼ cup water into a small bowl and sprinkle in ½ teaspoon sugar and yeast. Allow to sit 5 minutes.

2. In the bowl of a stand mixer, add 3 cups flour, remaining 1 cup water, salt, and remaining 1 tablespoon sugar. Using the flat beater attachment, mix well. Add in yeast mixture, then add remaining 1 cup flour. Switch to dough hook attachment and knead 5 minutes.

3. Preheat oven to 400°F. Line an ungreased baking sheet with parchment paper and set aside.

4. Cut dough into eight equal chunks. Roll each chunk between your hands to create a breadstick about 8" long. Place on prepared baking sheet and shape like an *S*. Let sit 15 minutes.

5. In a small bowl, mix butter and garlic together. Brush over each breadstick. Sprinkle cheese on top of each breadstick and press lightly to adhere.

6. Bake until golden brown, about 15 minutes. Store any leftovers in a sealed plastic bag in the refrigerator up to 3 days.

Hummus Trio

Adventureland, Disneyland

· · · · ✦ · · ·

Bengal Barbecue might be known for its Jungle Skewers and barbecued treats, but for a healthier, fresher snack, check out the Hummus Trio, and serve with a side of fresh vegetables. If you find yourself missing some of those familiar flavors (but don't have the time or energy to step up to the grill), this incredibly quick and easy recipe has you covered. Make these in big batches and portion them into little jars or plastic containers for a healthy snack on the go.

YIELDS 1½ PINTS EACH TYPE

For Black Bean Hummus

1 teaspoon minced garlic

1 (15-ounce) can black beans, drained but not rinsed

2 tablespoons lime juice

1 ½ tablespoons tahini

1 teaspoon ground cumin

1 teaspoon salt

½ teaspoon paprika

Put all ingredients in a blender or food processor and blend until creamy. Store in an airtight jar or plastic container in the refrigerator up to 7 days.

For Roasted Red Pepper and Feta Hummus

1 (15-ounce) can chickpeas, drained but not rinsed

½ cup crumbled feta cheese

1 (4-ounce) can roasted red peppers, drained

3 tablespoons lemon juice

1 tablespoon dried parsley

½ teaspoon salt

2 tablespoons tahini

Put all ingredients in a blender or food processor and blend until creamy. Store in an airtight jar or plastic container in the refrigerator up to 7 days.

(continued) ▶

For Roasted Jalapeño and Garlic Hummus

2 large jalapeño peppers
5 medium cloves garlic, unpeeled
2 tablespoons olive oil
1 (15-ounce) can chickpeas, drained but not rinsed
½ cup tahini
4 tablespoons lime juice
1 teaspoon lemon juice
1 teaspoon ground cumin
1 teaspoon salt
1 tablespoon dried cilantro

1. Preheat oven to 425°F.

2. Place jalapeños and garlic on a baking sheet lined with aluminum foil. Drizzle garlic with olive oil. Roast 10 minutes. Remove garlic and place on cutting board and flip the jalapeños. Roast jalapeños an additional 5 minutes. Remove from oven and immediately wrap in aluminum foil to steam 5 minutes.

3. In a blender or food processor, add remaining ingredients. Peel garlic, chop coarsely, and add to blender. Unwrap jalapeños and pull off skin and remove seeds. Coarsely chop and add to blender, starting with one pepper and adding more to reach your desired spice level.

4. Blend until smooth, or with some chunks remaining if desired. Store in an airtight jar or plastic container in the refrigerator up to 7 days.

DID YOU KNOW?

In 2019, Disney Parks committed to serving more vegetarian, vegan, and allergy-friendly meals, including offering Impossible Burger, a plant-based beef substitute.

Pork Belly Skewers

Adventureland, Disneyland

· · · ✦ · · ·

Have you ever taken a Pork Belly Skewer aboard the Jungle Cruise? It's like dinner and a show! Trainee Jungle Cruise Skippers are given a packet of jokes dozens of pages long to study in preparation for their job. Situational jokes are also learned, like if it is raining or if there are an abundance of ducks on the river. Whip up these savory skewers for your next meal and challenge your family to come up with their own jokes worthy of the Disneyland cruise.

SERVES 6

12 (8") wooden skewers
2 pounds pork belly, cut into
  1" cubes
½ cup hoisin sauce

1. Soak wooden skewers in water 30 minutes. Preheat grill or grill pan 10 minutes to high heat.

2. Place about seven pork pieces on each skewer with a ½" space between each piece. Use a kitchen brush to brush hoisin sauce generously over pork.

3. Grill skewers until completely cooked through, about 8 minutes.

Safari Skewers

Adventureland, Disneyland

· · · ✦ · · ·

Bengal Barbecue used to be a juice bar called "Sunkist, I Presume" back when it opened in 1962, due to Sunkist's sponsorship. However, Sunkist decided not to renew its sponsorship in 1990, and the modern Bengal Barbecue was born. What used to be only a juice bar now has a wide selection of meat and vegetable choices to choose from. The combination of rich meat and fresh vegetables in this dish makes it a Bengal Barbecue favorite.

SERVES 6

6 (8") wooden skewers
½ pound thick-cut bacon, cut into 2" strips
8 thick spears asparagus, cut into 1" pieces

1. Soak wooden skewers in water 30 minutes. Preheat grill or grill pan 10 minutes to medium-high heat.

2. Wrap each bacon strip around a piece of asparagus. Spear a skewer into the horizontal side of asparagus piece right at bacon edge. Repeat with remaining wrapped asparagus pieces and skewers, dividing asparagus evenly among skewers.

3. Grill skewers until bacon is cooked through and asparagus is tender, about 8 minutes.

Beignets

New Orleans Square, Disneyland

· · · ✦ · · ·

Beignets (pronounced ben-YAYS) originated in France and were brought over to Louisiana with the French settlers. Eating these pillowy doughnuts was (and is!) an integral part of any Mardi Gras celebration. New Orleans Square's seasonal Beignet flavors include Hot Chocolate, Candy Cane, Pumpkin, Gingerbread, and even Bubblegum. The Bubblegum Beignets were sold as an exclusive treat at a Disneyland After Dark: 80s Nite event.

SERVES 10

1½ cups warm water (110°F)

½ cup granulated sugar

1 (¼-ounce) packet active dry yeast

2 large eggs

1¼ teaspoons salt

1 cup evaporated milk

7 cups bread flour, divided

¼ cup shortening

4 cups vegetable oil for frying

3 cups confectioners' sugar

1. In a small bowl, stir water together with sugar and yeast. Let sit 10 minutes.

2. In the bowl of a stand mixer, add eggs. Using the whisk attachment, beat eggs 1 minute. Add salt and evaporated milk. Add yeast mixture and combine.

3. Add 3 cups flour while continuing to mix. Add shortening until combined. Add remaining flour until thoroughly combined.

4. Switch to dough hook attachment and knead until dough comes together, about 5 minutes.

5. Grease a separate large bowl with nonstick cooking spray. Transfer dough to greased bowl. Place plastic wrap greased with cooking spray over top of bowl and let rise 3 hours at room temperature.

6. In a large, heavy-bottomed pot over medium heat, add vegetable oil. It should measure to a depth of about 2". Heat until oil reaches 350°F. Line a large plate with paper towels and set aside.

(continued) ▶

7. Flour a flat surface and roll dough out to ¼" thickness. Cut into Mickey shapes (or shape into Mickey face by hand).

8. Carefully slide two or three dough Mickeys into the hot oil and fry about 1 minute on each side, until golden brown. Transfer to lined plate. Repeat with remaining dough.

9. Allow fried Beignets to drain 30 seconds, then pile high with confectioners' sugar.

DID YOU KNOW?

Beignets got their Disney fame from the animated motion picture The Princess and the Frog. *Tiana was hired by her debutant friend, Charlotte La Bouff, to make huge amounts of "man fetchin' beignets" for her Mardi Gras party. Now you can fetch whomever you want when you make these at home!*

Fritters

New Orleans Square, Disneyland

· · · · ✦ · · ·

These fritters were sold at Disneyland many years ago. They have since been replaced by seasonal offerings, such as Double Chocolate Fritters and Berry Cheesecake Fritters. Now you can enjoy the original right at home!

SERVES 6

4 cups vegetable oil for frying
¼ cup cold salted butter
1 cup boiling water
1 cup all-purpose flour
½ teaspoon salt
4 large eggs
1 cup granulated sugar

1. In a large pot over medium-high heat, add vegetable oil to reach a depth of about 3". Heat until oil reaches 375°F.

2. In a medium saucepan over medium heat, add butter, water, flour, and salt. Stir continuously until a smooth ball forms and dough pulls away from the sides of the pan, about 4 minutes. Remove from heat and allow to cool 10 minutes.

3. Scoop dough into a food processor fitted with a metal blade. Add eggs one at a time, pulsing between each addition to mix thoroughly.

4. Line a large plate with paper towels and set aside. Pour sugar into a medium bowl and set aside.

5. Once oil is heated, dip a spoon or 2-tablespoon cookie scoop into hot oil, then use that spoon to carefully scoop dough from food processor and drop into oil. Repeat twice and cook fritters 4 minutes, until deep golden brown.

6. Remove cooked fritters from oil with tongs or a slotted spoon and place on lined plate. Repeat with remaining dough.

7. While still hot, roll fritters in sugar. Enjoy immediately.

DID YOU KNOW?

This type of fried dough is typically called choux pastry, *pronounced "shoe."* Fritter *sounds a lot more appetizing!*

Clam Chowder

New Orleans Square, Disneyland

Although Clam Chowder is a well-known bayou favorite, there are actually only two main varieties: New England Clam Chowder and Manhattan Clam Chowder. The New England style has a cream base, while the Manhattan version has a tomato sauce base. So, this recipe is considered a New England Clam Chowder, even though it is served in "New Orleans Square" at Disneyland. The sounds of Pirates of the Caribbean are available online—play them in your kitchen as you eat this delicious Clam Chowder.

SERVES 8

⅓ cup cold salted butter

⅓ cup all-purpose flour

2 tablespoons vegetable oil

2 large yellow potatoes, peeled and diced

1 medium white onion, peeled and diced

2 medium stalks celery, trimmed and diced

1 cup clam juice

1½ cups heavy cream

2 (8-ounce) cans chopped clams in juice

1 teaspoon ground thyme

½ teaspoon salt

⅛ teaspoon ground white pepper

1. In a small saucepan over medium heat, melt butter, then mix in flour. Continue to cook, stirring frequently, 5 minutes. Remove from heat and set aside.

2. In a large pot over medium heat, add oil and heat 30 seconds. Then add potatoes, onion, and celery. Cook about 10 minutes, until onion is translucent.

3. Add clam juice, cream, canned clams including juice, thyme, salt, white pepper, and butter mixture. Stir to combine and bring to a boil. Reduce heat to a simmer and cook 5 minutes, until potatoes are soft.

4. Store leftovers in an airtight container in the refrigerator up to 3 days.

Mint Juleps

New Orleans Square, Disneyland

· · · ✳ · · ·

The Mint Julep is the official drink of the Kentucky Derby, and as many as 120,000 Mint Juleps are enjoyed on Derby Day in Kentucky each year. Typically, the drink is made with bourbon, but Disneyland Parks are traditionally alcohol-free. The exceptions to this rule are at the exclusive Club 33 and Oga's Cantina in Star Wars: Galaxy's Edge.

SERVES 2

For Mint Syrup

1 cup granulated sugar
1 cup room-temperature water
1 tablespoon mint extract

In a medium microwave-safe bowl, combine sugar, water, and mint extract. Microwave on high 1 minute, stir, then microwave 1 minute more. Stir, cover, and refrigerate at least 1 hour.

For Juleps

1 cup lemonade
1 cup club soda
4 tablespoons Mint Syrup
4 maraschino cherries
2 fresh mint leaves

1. For each Julep, fill a highball glass with ice. Pour ½ cup lemonade and ½ cup club soda over ice. Add 2 tablespoons Mint Syrup and stir. (Reserve remaining syrup for another use. Store in an airtight container in the refrigerator up to 2 weeks.)

2. Skewer 2 cherries and 1 mint leaf with a toothpick to garnish each drink.

MIX IT UP

Not a fan of mint? Not a problem! Try making this recipe with a different extract flavor. Some fun ideas include orange, strawberry, vanilla, and cherry.

Gold Port Galley Lemonade

Critter Country, Disneyland

· · · · ✦ · · · ·

This is a delicious and refreshing alternative to traditional summer drinks. Instead of serving regular lemonade or fruit punch at your next barbecue or pool party, whip this up! For a shortcut when you're pressed for time, use premade lemonade and just mix in the passion fruit–flavored syrup before starting up the ice cream machine.

SERVES 6

1¾ cups granulated sugar
8 cups room-temperature water, divided
1½ cups lemon juice
2 tablespoons passion fruit–flavored syrup
½ cup candied pineapple, chopped

1. In a large microwave-safe bowl, combine sugar and 1 cup water. Microwave on high 1 minute, stir, and microwave another minute. Refrigerate syrup covered until cool, about 2 hours.

2. Once cool, stir in lemon juice, remaining 7 cups water, and passion fruit flavoring. Pour into ice cream machine and mix about 15 minutes or until a slushy consistency forms.

3. Scoop into glasses and top with candied pineapple. Save any remaining lemonade to freeze another day, or drink unfrozen. Store in a pitcher in the refrigerator up to 5 days.

Churro Funnel Cake

Critter Country, Disneyland

· · · · ✦ · · ·

Churro Funnel Cake is a delicious treat to nosh on while sitting in the serenity that is Critter Country. Imagineers wanted to create Winnie-the-Pooh attractions at Walt Disney World and Disneyland but knew they would have to remove an old attraction from each park to make room. Fans rose up in outrage, demanding the classic attractions stay put. Imagineers decided to listen and compromise: Mr. Toad's Wild Ride was removed from Walt Disney World but remained at Disneyland. Bring some of this nostalgia into your own kitchen with this easy treat!

SERVES 4

- 4 cups vegetable oil for frying
- 1½ cups whole milk
- 2 large eggs
- 2 cups all-purpose flour
- 1 teaspoon baking powder
- 2 teaspoons plus 1 tablespoon ground cinnamon, divided
- ½ teaspoon salt
- ¼ cup granulated sugar
- ½ cup caramel sauce
- ½ cup whipped cream

1. In a large, heavy-bottomed pot over medium-high heat, add vegetable oil. Heat until oil reaches 375°F. Line a large plate with paper towels and set aside.

2. In a large bowl, whisk together milk and eggs until well combined. Then add flour, baking powder, 2 teaspoons cinnamon, and salt. Batter should be slightly thinner than pancake batter.

3. Add ½ cup batter to a funnel (or spouted measuring cup), keeping narrow end closed. Starting in the center of the oil, pour batter slowly from the narrow end of the funnel while spiraling outward. Cook 2 minutes per side or until golden brown.

4. Move cake to lined plate to drain, then place on another large clean plate.

5. In a small bowl, mix together sugar and remaining 1 table-spoon cinnamon. Dust over funnel cake. Drizzle with caramel sauce. Squirt whipped cream into a Mickey shape.

The Grey Stuff Gâteau

Fantasyland, Disneyland

· · · ✦ · · ·

The Red Rose Taverne at Disneyland opened in response to the 2017 live-action adaptation of *Beauty and the Beast*. The Grey Stuff Gâteau, named for the "gray stuff" served to Belle in the animated film, soon became its most popular item. This delectable treat sets itself apart from the Walt Disney World dish by adding a shortbread cookie base and fruit and cake interior. Serve up as a surprise dessert to make any dinner magical.

SERVES 12

For Shortbread Cookies

1 cup salted butter, softened
½ cup plus 2 tablespoons granulated sugar, divided
1 teaspoon vanilla extract
2 cups all-purpose flour

1. Preheat oven to 350°F. Line an ungreased baking sheet with parchment paper and set aside.

2. In the bowl of a stand mixer, add butter and ½ cup sugar. Using the flat beater attachment, cream together well, then add vanilla and flour. Mix until dough is sticking together but still crumbly, about 2 minutes. Form into a ball by hand.

3. Sprinkle 1 tablespoon sugar across a flat surface and place dough ball on it. Sprinkle the top with remaining 1 tablespoon sugar and roll dough out to ¼" thickness.

4. Using a biscuit cutter (or a drinking glass flipped upside down), cut out twelve 3" circles.

5. Carefully transfer dough circles onto prepared baking sheet. Bake about 12 minutes; they will look very light, with slight browning on the bottom. Allow to cool completely on baking sheet, about 1 hour.

For Red Velvet Cake

1 box red velvet cake mix, mixed according to package instructions
The Grey Stuff (see recipe in Chapter 4)
12 medium fresh raspberries

1. Pour prepared cake batter into a mini-muffin tin greased with nonstick cooking spray. Bake according to box instructions.

2. Allow to cool completely, about 1 hour, then remove mini-cupcakes from tin and place onto a baking rack.

3. To assemble: Spoon The Grey Stuff into a large piping bag fitted with a medium-large star tip. Lay out Shortbread Cookies. Place one red velvet mini-cupcake upside down onto each cookie. Trim a tiny bit off the bump side of cupcake if needed for it to sit flat. Place 1 fresh raspberry point side up on top of each cupcake. Pipe The Grey Stuff beginning at base of cupcake, swirling up and over the raspberry, ending at the top.

MIX IT UP

This recipe calls for red velvet cake, but if that's not your style, try mixing things up with a different flavor! A moist yellow or white cake would pair nicely with the rich cookies and cream flavor of The Grey Stuff.

Matterhorn Macaroons

Fantasyland, Disneyland

• • • ✦ • • •

The Matterhorn Bobsleds attraction at Disneyland was the first tubular roller coaster system in the world to send out more than one ride vehicle at a time. It opened in 1959, just four years after the original opening of Disneyland, and was part of the first major expansion of the park. The fictitious mountain stands at 147 feet—a perfect $\frac{1}{100}$ scale of the real Matterhorn mountain in Switzerland. These cute little treats are designed to look like mini Matterhorns, complete with "snowcapped" peaks!

SERVES 10

1 (14-ounce) package unsweetened shredded coconut

⅔ cup all-purpose flour

¼ teaspoon salt

1 (12-ounce) can sweetened condensed milk

2 cups white chocolate chips, divided

1. Preheat oven to 350°F. Line an ungreased baking sheet with parchment paper and set aside.

2. In a large bowl, stir together coconut, flour, and salt. Add condensed milk and stir until well combined.

3. Wet hands with water and scoop up about ½ cup dough. Form into a mountain shape, then place on prepared baking sheet. Continue with remaining dough, wetting hands between each macaroon, and leaving a 1" space between each on the baking sheet.

4. Bake until coconut is browning, about 15 minutes. Allow to cool completely, about 20 minutes, on baking sheet.

5. In a medium microwave-safe bowl, add 1¾ cups chocolate chips. Microwave on high 30 seconds, stir, then microwave another 15 seconds. Repeat microwaving in 15-second increments, stirring between each, until white chocolate just melts.

6. Chop remaining ¼ cup chocolate chips roughly with a knife.

7. Once macaroons are cool, dip each macaroon one at a time into melted white chocolate to make a snowy "peak," then sprinkle with chopped white chocolate.

Brownie Bites

Tomorrowland, Disneyland

· · · ✦ · · ·

Many of the attractions and food locations at Disney Parks have elaborate fictitious histories that most people never even hear about. For the Pizza Port (later rethemed Alien Pizza Planet)—the restaurant that used to serve Brownie Bites—it's the story of a space traveler named Redd Rockett who was so fed up with the inaccessibility of good food in the galaxy that he decided to start his own pizza parlor.
Luckily, you can now enjoy them right at home!

YIELDS 24 BITES

½ cup salted butter, softened
1 cup granulated sugar
2 large eggs
1 teaspoon vanilla extract
½ cup cocoa powder
½ cup all-purpose flour
¼ teaspoon salt
¼ teaspoon baking powder
½ cup confectioners' sugar

1. Preheat oven to 350°F. Line an 8" × 5" baking dish with parchment paper, allowing about 2" overhang on all sides. Set aside.

2. In the bowl of a stand mixer, add butter, sugar, eggs, and vanilla. Using the flat beater attachment, cream together well. Add cocoa powder, flour, salt, and baking powder, and stir until combined.

3. Scoop batter into prepared dish. Bake 30 minutes, or until toothpick inserted in the center comes out clean.

4. Allow to cool completely in dish, about 1 hour. Once cooled, lift up the parchment paper to remove brownies from the pan. Cut brownies into 1" cubes.

5. Pour confectioners' sugar into a paper lunch bag and put about 4 brownie cubes into the bag. Shake gently to coat in confectioners' sugar. Repeat until all brownies are coated. Store in an airtight container at room temperature up to 3 days.

DID YOU KNOW?

Brownies are a fairly common dessert at the Disney Parks, but Pizza Port was the only place where you could get these far-out cube brownies covered in delicious confectioners' sugar!

CHAPTER 4

Magic Kingdom

At first glance, Disneyland and Magic Kingdom have a lot of similarities; the fun is finding the differences! Gaston's Tavern in Fantasyland is unique to Magic Kingdom and has its own *Beauty and the Beast* offerings like Gaston's Giant Cinnamon Rolls and LeFou's Brew. Sleepy Hollow in Liberty Square serves up waffles with toppings that range from the classic, like Nutella with fresh fruit, to the intriguing, like spicy chicken with arugula. And don't forget about Loaded Buffalo Chicken Tots from The Friar's Nook! Discovering new food favorites is just as fun as hopping on a thrill ride. In fact, some attractions can be enhanced by a recipe. Did you know you can enjoy a Dole Whip while at Walt Disney's Enchanted Tiki Room? Or that snacks are allowed in most ride queues? If you have to stand in line for an hour, you might as well be holding a Turkey Leg, right? Of course, thanks to this chapter, you don't have to wait for a trip to Magic Kingdom to enjoy any of these mouthwatering creations. Bring a little Disney magic to your dinner table, friend gathering, or wherever you choose!

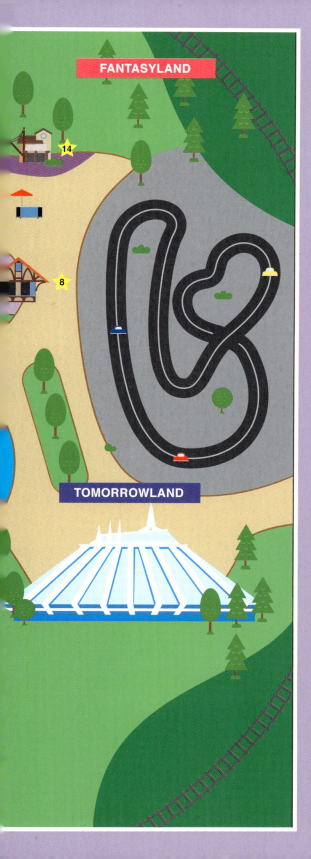

⭐ **1** **MICKEY SUGAR COOKIES** *(Main Street, U.S.A., Magic Kingdom)*

⭐ **2** **CARAMEL APPLES** *(Main Street, U.S.A., Magic Kingdom)*

⭐ **3** **BACON MACARONI & CHEESE HOT DOGS** *(Main Street, U.S.A., Magic Kingdom)*

⭐ **4** **CORN DOG NUGGETS** *(Main Street, U.S.A., Magic Kingdom)*

⭐ **5** **SWEET-AND-SPICY CHICKEN WAFFLE SANDWICHES** *(Liberty Square, Magic Kingdom)*

⭐ **6** **FUNNEL CAKE** *(Liberty Square, Magic Kingdom)*

⭐ **7** **FRESH FRUIT WAFFLE SANDWICHES** *(Liberty Square, Magic Kingdom)*

⭐ **8** **CHESHIRE CAT TAILS** *(Fantasyland, Magic Kingdom)*

⭐ **9** **LEFOU'S BREW** *(Fantasyland, Magic Kingdom)*

⭐ **10** **THE GREY STUFF** *(Fantasyland, Magic Kingdom)*

⭐ **11** **GASTON'S GIANT CINNAMON ROLLS** *(Fantasyland, Magic Kingdom)*

⭐ **12** **PETER PAN FLOATS** *(Fantasyland, Magic Kingdom)*

⭐ **13** **TOMATO BASIL SOUP** *(Fantasyland, Magic Kingdom)*

⭐ **14** **TURKEY LEGS** *(Fantasyland, Magic Kingdom)*

⭐ **15** **LOADED BUFFALO CHICKEN TOTS** *(Fantasyland, Magic Kingdom)*

⭐ **16** **CHEESEBURGER SPRING ROLLS** *(Adventureland, Magic Kingdom)*

⭐ **17** **PIZZA SPRING ROLLS** *(Adventureland, Magic Kingdom)*

⭐ **18** **DOLE WHIP** *(Adventureland, Magic Kingdom)*

⭐ **19** **PINEAPPLE UPSIDE DOWN CAKE** *(Adventureland, Magic Kingdom)*

⭐ **20** **MAPLE POPCORN** *(Frontierland, Magic Kingdom)*

Mickey Sugar Cookies

Main Street, U.S.A., Magic Kingdom

· · · · ✦ · · ·

When these cookies are baking in the oven, it will be hard *not* to think of the Magic Kingdom! Main Street, U.S.A., smells sweet not only because there is a bakery, but also because Disney is actually pumping vanilla scent into the air. Several attractions also use smells to enhance their experience, like oranges and sea salt on Soarin' (Disney California Adventure). The scents captivate our senses and create strong memory connections. You can use a cookie cutter to form the dough in this recipe into Mickey Mouse shapes before baking.

YIELDS 3 DOZEN COOKIES

1 cup rainbow sprinkles
1½ cups salted butter, softened
1½ cups granulated sugar
2 large eggs
1 teaspoon vanilla extract
3¾ cups all-purpose flour
2 teaspoons baking powder
1 teaspoon salt

1. Preheat oven to 350°F. Place sprinkles in a small bowl and set aside. Line an ungreased baking sheet with parchment paper and set aside.

2. In the bowl of a stand mixer, add butter and sugar. Using the flat beater attachment, cream together well. Add eggs and vanilla and combine. Add flour, baking powder, and salt. Combine.

3. Scoop about 2 tablespoons dough into your hand and roll into a ball. Place on prepared baking sheet and flatten a little with the bottom of a glass. If you have a Mickey cookie cutter, use it now to make a Mickey shape, discarding the extra dough around the edges. Lightly dot top of cookie with sprinkles, pressing sprinkles into dough a bit. Repeat with remaining dough.

4. Bake until bottoms just barely brown, about 15 minutes.

5. Allow to cool slightly on the sheet, about 10 minutes, before moving cookies to a cooling rack. Store leftovers in an airtight container at room temperature for up to 5 days.

Caramel Apples

Main Street, U.S.A., Magic Kingdom

· · · · ✦ · · ·

There is no place better than Main Street, U.S.A., to indulge in a Caramel Apple. You can feel like a kid again, biting into the juicy, sweet apple while watching a parade go by. And the best part about Disney Parks' Caramel Apples are the toppings: Choices include M&M's, Reese's Peanut Butter Cups, sprinkles, peanut butter chips, pecans, and more. You can even get themed apples (which are usually seasonal), like a "poison apple," Mickey Jack-o'-Lantern, Cinderella's Carriage, Goofy, and more. Try some of these decoration ideas on your Caramel Apples at home!

SERVES 6

6 large Granny Smith apples
1 (11-ounce) package soft
  caramels, unwrapped
2 tablespoons whole milk

1. Prepare your countertop with a piece of parchment paper greased with nonstick cooking spray. Set aside.

2. Push a Popsicle stick deep into the stem area of each apple. Set aside.

3. In a medium microwave-safe bowl, add caramels and milk. Microwave on high for 30 seconds. Stir. Microwave another 15 seconds. Stir. Repeat cooking in 15-second intervals and stirring until all caramels have melted.

4. Working with one apple at a time, roll the apple in the caramel to coat the whole apple. Place on greased parchment paper.

5. Allow Caramel Apples to set about 15 minutes before serving.

Bacon Macaroni & Cheese Hot Dogs

Main Street, U.S.A., Magic Kingdom

· · · · ✦ · · ·

At the opening of Walt Disney World in 1971, Casey's Corner was originally named Coca-Cola Refreshment Corner. It was renamed in 1995 after the popular poem "Casey at the Bat" by Ernest Lawrence Thayer. The interior boasts a unifying baseball theme with a ragtime piano player out front—the perfect setting for this nostalgic ball game favorite! Bring the game to your own home with the following easy recipe.

SERVES 12

- 3 tablespoons cold salted butter
- 2 tablespoons all-purpose flour
- 2 cups whole milk
- 2 cups shredded sharp Cheddar cheese
- 2 cups elbow pasta, cooked and drained
- 1½ teaspoons salt
- 1 teaspoon ground black pepper
- 12 beef hot dogs
- 12 hot dog buns
- ½ cup precooked bacon bits

1. In a large saucepan over low heat, melt butter. Add flour and cook 2 minutes, stirring continually. Raise heat to medium and add milk. Bring to a boil while continuing to stir. Once it reaches boiling, lower heat and simmer 4 minutes.

2. Add cheese to saucepan and stir until melted and well combined. Pour in cooked pasta and stir until coated. Sprinkle with salt and pepper.

3. Grill hot dogs over medium heat about 5 minutes, or to desired doneness, then place in buns. Spoon a generous amount of macaroni & cheese on top of each dog and garnish with bacon bits.

MIX IT UP

Other hot dogs on the menu at Casey's Corner include a Chili-Cheese Dog and Loaded Slaw Dog. Get creative! Try topping with a dill pickle spear, or maybe sprinkling on crushed potato chips! Make your hot dog a meal to remember.

Corn Dog Nuggets

Main Street, U.S.A., Magic Kingdom

· · · · ✦ · · ·

If you have the weird sensation of being more kid-sized while on Main Street, U.S.A., you're not crazy. It's a tactic called "forced perspective." The buildings actually get smaller at the tops, making the viewer feel little and the buildings feel even bigger. Eating kid-food staples like these Corn Dog Nuggets has the same effect of transporting you back to childhood. Pair with your favorite dipping sauces and enjoy as either a snack or part of a full meal.

SERVES 10

4 cups vegetable oil for frying
16 beef hot dogs, cut crosswise into thirds
1 cup yellow cornmeal
1 cup all-purpose flour
1¼ cups whole milk
½ cup granulated sugar
½ teaspoon salt
½ teaspoon ground black pepper
4 teaspoons baking powder
1 large egg

1. In a large, heavy-bottomed pot over medium-high heat, add vegetable oil. It should measure to a depth of about 3". Heat until oil reaches 350°F. Line a large plate with paper towels and set aside.

2. Pat hot dog pieces dry with a paper towel.

3. In the bowl of a stand mixer, add remaining ingredients. Using the flat beater attachment, beat until well combined.

4. Working with one hot dog piece at a time, dunk into batter and carefully place into hot oil. You can fry up to five hot dog pieces at one time. Allow to cook about 2 minutes, making sure to cook all sides evenly, until golden brown.

5. Remove to lined plate. Repeat with remaining hot dog pieces.

Sweet-and-Spicy
Chicken Waffle Sandwiches

Liberty Square, Magic Kingdom

· · · ✦ · · ·

Sleepy Hollow serves these scrumptious savory-sweet snacks and is located close to Cinderella Castle. This waffle sandwich is the best of all worlds: The crisp waffle, plus the sticky-sweet sauce with a slight kick, is sure to please everyone, from family to party guests.

SERVES 6

For Chicken

4 cups vegetable oil for frying
1½ cups all-purpose flour
1 teaspoon salt
1 teaspoon ground black pepper
1 teaspoon onion powder
1 teaspoon garlic powder
1 large egg
1 tablespoon room-temperature water
1½ pounds boneless, skinless chicken breast, cut into 1"-thick strips

1. Preheat oven to 170°F.

2. In a large, heavy-bottomed pot over medium heat, add vegetable oil. It should measure to a depth of 2". Heat until oil reaches 340°F.

3. In a medium shallow bowl, stir together flour, salt, pepper, onion powder, and garlic powder. In a separate shallow bowl, mix egg and water together.

4. Dredge each chicken strip in flour mixture, then egg mixture, then flour mixture again. Place on a large plate and allow to rest 5 minutes.

5. Line a separate large plate with paper towels and set aside.

6. Carefully lower five strips into the hot oil one at a time and allow to fry until internal temperature is at least 165°F, about 8 minutes. Remove from oil onto lined plate. Repeat with remaining chicken strips.

(continued) ▶

For Spicy-Sweet Sauce

2 tablespoons salted butter, melted
2 tablespoons sriracha sauce
2 tablespoons pulp-free orange juice
¼ cup pure maple syrup
¼ cup sweet chili sauce
1 tablespoon amber honey

In a large bowl, mix together butter, sriracha, orange juice, maple syrup, sweet chili sauce, and honey. Set aside until ready to assemble sandwiches.

For Sandwiches

6 Mickey Waffles (see recipe in Chapter 7)
2 cups fresh coleslaw mix
2 tablespoons coleslaw dressing
½ cup fresh arugula leaves

1. In a medium bowl, combine coleslaw mix and coleslaw dressing.

2. Top one Mickey Waffle (made with a standard circular waffle maker) with ¼ cup coleslaw mixture. Toss Chicken in the Spicy-Sweet Sauce to coat. Top coleslaw with one-sixth of the Chicken. Top with a bit of arugula. Fold into a taco shape. Repeat with remaining ingredients.

Funnel Cake

Liberty Square, Magic Kingdom

· · · ✦ · · ·

The first Funnel Cake dates back to 1879, where it was believed to have been cooked up by Pennsylvania Germans. Now, Funnel Cakes are not only a staple at theme parks, state fairs, and carnivals, but several countries have their own version of the treat. The Liberty Square version, keeping in theme with the rest of the square, is an ode to the classic American serving style.

SERVES 4

4 cups vegetable oil for frying
1½ cups whole milk
2 large eggs
2 cups all-purpose flour
1 tablespoon baking powder
2 tablespoons ground cinnamon
½ teaspoon salt
½ cup confectioners' sugar

1. In a large pot over medium-high heat, add vegetable oil to reach a depth of about 3". Heat until oil reaches 375°F. Line a large plate with paper towels and set aside.

2. In a large bowl, whisk together milk and eggs until well combined. Then add flour, baking powder, cinnamon, and salt. Batter should be slightly thinner than pancake batter.

3. Add ½ cup batter to a funnel (or spouted measuring cup), keeping narrow end closed. Starting in the center of the oil, pour batter slowly from the narrow end of the funnel while spiraling outward. Cook 3 minutes per side or until golden brown.

4. Move Funnel Cake to lined plate to drain, then place on a serving plate.

5. Generously sprinkle confectioners' sugar over top while still hot.

MIX IT UP

Try different toppings, like chocolate sauce, fresh strawberries, or scoops of ice cream. Some Funnel Cakes are even served with a "slab" of ice cream. You can do this yourself by taking a frozen rectangular half gallon of ice cream immediately from the freezer and slicing through the block in a straight line. Plop onto your hot Funnel Cake and you're good to go!

Fresh Fruit Waffle Sandwiches

Liberty Square, Magic Kingdom

· · · · ✦ · · ·

Residents of the real colonial America certainly did not have access to chocolate-hazelnut spread, but guests to Liberty Square won't mind a deviation from authenticity to indulge in this treat. And do you have a jar of chocolate-hazelnut spread in your pantry that is almost gone after making this recipe? Here's a fun idea: Scoop vanilla ice cream into the almost-empty jar and eat the ice cream straight out of it. It will perfectly flavor your ice cream while using up each and every delicious dollop of leftover spread.

SERVES 6

6 Mickey Waffles (see recipe in Chapter 7)
½ cup chocolate-hazelnut spread
2 large ripe bananas, peeled and sliced
2 cups strawberries, hulled and sliced
1 cup fresh blueberries

Spread Mickey Waffles (made with a standard circular waffle maker) with chocolate-hazelnut spread. Top with bananas, strawberries, and blueberries. Repeat with remaining waffles and other ingredients. Fold waffles in half into sandwiches to serve.

Cheshire Cat Tails

Fantasyland, Magic Kingdom

· · · · ✦ · · ·

The Cheshire Cat is a popular character from Lewis Carroll's book *Alice's Adventures in Wonderland*, known for his crazy personality and antics. And this colorful pastry treat was created after him! Take a trip down the rabbit hole for dessert or host your own Wonderland party.

SERVES 6

For Pastries

1 (17.3-ounce) box frozen puff pastry sheets

1 (3.4-ounce) package instant vanilla pudding

1¾ cups whole milk

1 cup mini semisweet chocolate chips

1 large egg

1 tablespoon room-temperature water

1. Remove puff pastry from freezer and allow to thaw at room temperature 45 minutes. Preheat oven to 400°F. Line an ungreased baking sheet with parchment paper and set aside.

2. In a medium bowl, whisk together instant vanilla pudding and milk. Cover and chill in refrigerator until ready to use, at least 10 minutes.

3. Unfold both sheets puff pastry and use a rolling pin to just barely soften each surface. (Don't work the dough too much or it won't puff up in the oven.)

4. Spread a very thin layer of vanilla pudding onto each sheet of pastry and sprinkle one sheet with mini chocolate chips. Carefully lay the other sheet pudding-side down onto the mini chocolate chips.

5. Carefully cut the stacked pastry into six long strips. Holding a strip in your hand, twist one end. Lay on prepared baking sheet. Repeat with remaining strips.

6. In a small bowl, beat egg and water together. Brush mixture over tops of pastry.

7. Bake until golden brown and puffing up, about 20 minutes. Remove from oven and allow to cool completely, about 30 minutes, on baking sheet.

For Icing

1 cup confectioners' sugar
¼ cup heavy cream
1 teaspoon vanilla extract
2 drops purple gel food coloring
2 drops pink gel food coloring

In a medium bowl or stand mixer, mix together confectioners' sugar, cream, and vanilla. Divide evenly between two small bowls, and add one shade of food coloring to each bowl, stirring to combine well. Using a spoon or piping bag, drizzle both colors of icing over each twist.

COOKING TIP

A handy trick to bring your eggs to room temperature quickly: Fill a bowl with hot tap water and add the eggs to it. Allow them to sit in the hot water 3–5 minutes. Now you're ready to use the room-temperature eggs!

LeFou's Brew

Fantasyland, Magic Kingdom

· · · ✦ · · ·

One of the most popular character meet-and-greets in all of the Disney Parks is with Gaston. He is most often found near Gaston's Tavern, where LeFou's Brew is sold. Why is he such a favorite? Unlike most things at Disney, Gaston has a markedly *naughty* demeanor. He has no problem telling you that you could never beat him in a weight-lifting contest. This drink is so sweet and fruity it might embolden you to say something naughty too!

SERVES 6

1 cup heavy cream
3 tablespoons mango juice
3 tablespoons passion fruit juice
¼ cup confectioners' sugar
1 (12-ounce) can frozen apple juice concentrate
3 cups cold water
3 tablespoons toasted marshmallow syrup

1. In the bowl of a stand mixer, add cream, mango juice, passion fruit juice, and confectioners' sugar. Using the whisk attachment, whip until soft peaks form. Cover and refrigerate fruit foam while completing next steps.

2. In a large bowl, mix apple juice concentrate with water. Add marshmallow syrup. Pour into an ice cream machine. Follow manufacturer's instructions and run 20 minutes.

3. Scoop the mixture into glasses and top with fruit foam. Stir a bit to blend the flavors before serving.

The Grey Stuff

Fantasyland, Magic Kingdom

Beauty and the Beast is set in pre-revolutionary France, and it is likely that the "gray stuff" in the original film was a liver pâté of some sort. But Walt Disney World decided to make it into a sweet treat. It is served at Be Our Guest Restaurant, located way in the back of Magic Kingdom in Fantasyland. It's easy to think this restaurant is a ride because of the usually huge line snaking out of it. Inside are three themed dining rooms: the Grand Ballroom, the Castle Gallery, and the West Wing. Each room provides a unique dining ambiance.

SERVES 8

12 chocolate sandwich cookies
1 (3.4-ounce) box instant vanilla pudding
1½ cups whole milk
1 (8-ounce) tub frozen whipped topping, thawed

1. In a blender or food processor, crush chocolate sandwich cookies into a fine crumble. Set aside.

2. In a large bowl, add instant pudding powder and milk. Whisk together and let chill in refrigerator 10 minutes.

3. Stir in cookie crumbs and whipped topping with a spoon, being careful not to overmix.

Gaston's Giant Cinnamon Rolls

Fantasyland, Magic Kingdom

· · · · ✦ · · · ·

Disney Parks have sold cinnamon rolls for a long time—regular, boring-sized cinnamon rolls. But in 2012, they upped their cinnamon roll game when they introduced Gaston's Giant Cinnamon Rolls to their lineup . It is about 8" square in size and is smothered in frosting and butterscotch topping. It is perfectly made for the man who eats five dozen eggs each day—or your whole family!

SERVES 8

For Dough

½ cup salted butter, melted
1½ cups whole milk
6½ cups all-purpose flour, divided
2 (¼-ounce) packets active dry yeast
½ cup granulated sugar
1 teaspoon salt
½ cup room-temperature water
2 large eggs

1. Grease a 9" × 13" pan with nonstick cooking spray and set aside.

2. In a medium bowl, combine ½ cup melted butter and milk.

3. In the bowl of a stand mixer, add 2½ cups flour, yeast, sugar, and salt. Add water, eggs, and butter mixture. Using the flat beater attachment, mix until well combined. Add remaining flour ½ cup at a time while mixing until Dough starts to form a ball.

4. Switch to the dough hook attachment and knead Dough on low speed 5 minutes.

5. Remove Dough from bowl, sprinkle some flour in bowl, and place Dough back in the same bowl. Let rise 10 minutes in a warm place.

For Filling

2 cups light brown sugar
2 tablespoons ground cinnamon
1 cup salted butter, softened
¼ cup salted butter, melted

1. In a medium bowl, mix brown sugar, cinnamon, and softened butter together. Set aside.

2. Roll out Dough into a long rectangle, about 3' × 2'. Spread Filling evenly across the whole surface of the Dough.

(continued) ▶

Starting at short end, roll Dough like a jelly roll. Make a cut in the center of the roll, and then cut about 6" from the center on either side to make two giant rolls.

3. Place both rolls swirl-edge down in prepared pan.

4. Drizzle melted butter over rolls. Allow rolls to rise at room temperature 30 minutes.

5. Preheat oven to 375°F. Bake rolls 20 minutes, then cover loosely with foil and bake another 10 minutes.

For Cream Cheese Frosting

8 ounces cream cheese
¼ cup salted butter, softened
2 cups confectioners' sugar
1 teaspoon vanilla extract
3 tablespoons heavy cream
⅛ teaspoon salt

In a medium saucepan over medium heat, add cream cheese and butter. Combine and heat until melted, about 3 minutes. Remove from heat and stir in confectioners' sugar. Add vanilla, cream, and salt. Stir, then set aside.

For Butterscotch Topping

½ cup light brown sugar
4 tablespoons salted butter, softened
½ cup heavy cream
¼ teaspoon salt
1 teaspoon vanilla extract

1. In a separate medium saucepan over medium heat, add brown sugar, butter, and cream. Bring to a boil and boil 5 minutes, stirring frequently. Remove from heat. Add salt and vanilla. Set aside.

2. To serve, place each giant roll on a large plate. Drizzle Cream Cheese Frosting in one direction along each roll's swirl, then drizzle with Butterscotch Topping in the other direction.

COOKING TIP

The dough left over on either end of the giant rolls need not be wasted! Make cuts about 1"–2" along the extra dough. Lay swirl-side down in a glass 9" × 13" baking dish greased with nonstick cooking spray and bake about 20 minutes at 375°F or until golden brown and cooked through.

Peter Pan Floats

Fantasyland, Magic Kingdom

Walt Disney had a personal connection to the story of Peter Pan before making it into an animated film: He played Peter Pan in a school play. This delicious float came along much later, in the wake of the wildly popular Dole Whip Float also served at Magic Kingdom. The Walt Disney World version of the Peter Pan Float comes with a red milk chocolate feather on it—just like Peter himself wears in his cap!

SERVES 10

4 large egg yolks
2 large eggs
1¼ cups granulated sugar
1 tablespoon lemon juice
¾ cup lime juice
1¼ cups heavy cream
1¼ cups whole milk
2 liters lemon-lime soda

1. In a medium saucepan over medium heat, whisk together egg yolks, eggs, sugar, lemon juice, and lime juice. Cook 7 minutes, stirring continuously.

2. Strain mixture through a fine sieve into a large bowl. Add cream and milk. Stir to combine.

3. Refrigerate covered 1 hour.

4. Pour cooled mixture into an ice cream machine. Follow manufacturer's instructions and run about 20 minutes, or until mixture begins to thicken. Scoop into a large plastic container, cover, and freeze 5 hours or overnight.

5. To serve: Scoop ice cream into cups and pour lemon-lime soda on top.

Tomato Basil Soup

Fantasyland, Magic Kingdom

· · · ✦ · · ·

When you make Disney recipes at home, you can combine the impossible. This savory, filling tomato soup is even more delicious paired with a Tiger Tail Breadstick (see recipe in Chapter 3), but you can only get this winning combination in your own kitchen! Normally you would have to fly from Pinocchio Village Haus at Magic Kingdom in Florida to the Bengal Barbecue at Disneyland in California to enjoy these dishes together. Talk about kitchen magic!

SERVES 6

4 cups diced fresh Roma tomatoes
½ medium white onion, peeled and chopped
4 teaspoons minced garlic
2 cups chicken broth
2 tablespoons cold salted butter
2 tablespoons all-purpose flour
2 teaspoons salt
2 teaspoons granulated sugar
1 tablespoon Italian seasoning

1. In a large pot over medium heat, add tomatoes, onion, garlic, and broth. Cook 20 minutes.

2. Pour cooked tomato mixture into a blender (in batches if needed) or use an immersion blender. Blend until smooth. Set aside.

3. In a separate large pot over medium heat, add butter and flour. Stir and cook 4 minutes to make a roux. Add tomato mixture to roux one ladle at a time, whisking between each addition until all soup has been added.

4. Season with salt, sugar, and Italian seasoning. Stir until well combined. Serve immediately or store up to 5 days in a large sealed container in refrigerator.

Turkey Legs

Fantasyland, Magic Kingdom

· · · · ✦ · · · ·

A crazy rumor has been swirling around Disney Parks for years that the Turkey Legs are emu legs since they are so massive. This is not true! The Turkey Legs at Disney *are* unusually large, but this is because they come from only the largest turkeys available. Rest assured that the delicious meat you are snacking on is not exotic wildlife. Be it the circus tent across from The Barnstormer attraction or your own dining room, these Turkey Legs can be enjoyed just about anywhere.

SERVES 2

- 2 tablespoons salt
- 2 tablespoons light brown sugar
- 1 cup room-temperature water
- 2 (12-ounce) turkey drumsticks

1. Combine salt, brown sugar, and water in a large plastic zip-top bag. Add turkey drumsticks and allow to brine in the refrigerator 24 hours.

2. Preheat oven to 350°F. Place a wire cooling rack on top of a baking sheet.

3. Place drumsticks on cooling rack. Bake until internal temperature reaches 180°F, about 1 hour and 15 minutes.

4. Allow to cool 10 minutes on rack, then serve wrapped in wax paper.

Loaded Buffalo Chicken Tots

Fantasyland, Magic Kingdom

· · · ✦ · · ·

This dish hit the menu at The Friar's Nook in 2018, but this food location is no stranger to change. In fact, The Friar's Nook—which opened in 2009—is the sixth food establishment in that location at Magic Kingdom! If you look carefully at the restaurant's sign, you'll see the Roman numerals MLXXI, or 1071. This alludes to the opening of Magic Kingdom in October 1971. This filling, spicy treat has become a fan favorite that you can now enjoy for any meal or side right at home!

SERVES 3

- ½ (32-ounce) package frozen Tater Tots
- 1 cup shredded cooked chicken breast
- 1 tablespoon buffalo sauce
- 3 tablespoons blue cheese dressing
- 3 tablespoons blue cheese crumbles
- 2 medium stalks celery, trimmed and diced

1. Cook Tater Tots according to package instructions. Divide among three medium bowls. Set aside.

2. In a large bowl, toss chicken with buffalo sauce. Top each bowl with ⅓ buffalo chicken. Drizzle blue cheese dressing over top of each. Sprinkle on blue cheese crumbles and celery.

COOKING TIP

When heating the frozen tots in the oven, be sure to stir them on the baking sheet two to three times throughout the cooking process. This ensures an even browning. Often the suggested cook times on the back of the package are too short, so also make sure you check them for crispness before turning off the oven.

Cheeseburger Spring Rolls

Adventureland, Magic Kingdom

· · · · ✦ · · · ·

Like many snacks and treats at Disney Parks, these spring rolls (along with the Pizza Spring Rolls; see recipe in this chapter) have certainly garnered a cult following from fans. They showed up in Adventureland around 2015 but mysteriously stopped being served. In 2018 they reappeared in a larger size (and with a larger price tag). Making these spring rolls at home is both supereasy and cost-effective. Serve them with your favorite burger condiments!

YIELDS 10 ROLLS

1 tablespoon plus 2 cups vegetable oil, divided
½ medium yellow onion, peeled and diced
1 teaspoon minced garlic
1 pound ground beef
1 teaspoon salt
1 teaspoon ground black pepper
1 tablespoon yellow mustard
1 tablespoon ketchup
10 tablespoons shredded Cheddar cheese
10 egg roll wrappers
1 large egg, beaten

1. In a large skillet over medium heat, heat 1 tablespoon oil 30 seconds, then add onion and garlic. Cook 2 minutes. Add beef, salt, and pepper. Cook until beef is no longer pink, about 5 minutes.

2. Remove pan from heat and drain. Mix mustard and ketchup into beef mixture and allow to cool slightly, about 10 minutes. Set aside.

3. In a large, heavy-bottomed pot over medium-high heat, add remaining 2 cups vegetable oil. It should measure to a depth of about 1". Heat until oil reaches 350°F.

4. Line a large plate with paper towels and set aside.

5. Lay 1 egg roll wrapper with a point facing toward you. Spoon 2 tablespoons beef mixture onto middle of wrapper. Sprinkle 1 tablespoon cheese onto meat. Brush egg onto the opposite two sides of wrapper. Roll up like a burrito, making sure all filling is sealed inside. Repeat with remaining wraps and fillings.

6. Place 4 rolls in hot oil and cook 2 minutes per side, until golden brown. Remove to lined plate. Repeat with remaining rolls.

Pizza Spring Rolls

Adventureland, Magic Kingdom

· · · ✦ · · ·

Spring rolls originated in China, and eating one celebrates the advent of spring. The cylindrical shape and golden color are meant to symbolize gold bars, equating wealth. Filling them with pizza toppings is the perfect twist on the classic snack; after all, pizza wealth is the best kind of wealth!

YIELDS 10 ROLLS

2 cups vegetable oil for frying
2 cups shredded mozzarella cheese
½ cup pepperoni slices, quartered
½ cup pizza sauce
10 egg roll wrappers
1 large egg, beaten

1. In a large, heavy-bottomed pot over medium-high heat, add vegetable oil. It should measure to a depth of about 1". Heat until oil reaches 350°F.

2. Line a large plate with paper towels and set aside.

3. In a medium bowl, mix together cheese, pepperoni, and pizza sauce.

4. Lay an egg roll wrapper with a point facing toward you. Spoon 2 tablespoons filling onto middle of wrapper. Brush egg onto the opposite two sides of wrapper. Roll up like a burrito, making sure all filling is sealed inside. Repeat with remaining wraps and filling.

5. Place 4 rolls in hot oil and cook 2 minutes per side, until golden brown. Remove from oil and place on lined plate. Repeat with remaining rolls.

Dole Whip

Adventureland, Magic Kingdom

· · · · ✦ · · · ·

Dole Whip is arguably the number one cult classic favorite treat of all time at Disney Parks. This fruity-sweet snack began in Hawaii on the Dole Plantation, where parched tourists got to sample the sorbet after a walk around the pineapple bushes. Promoted alongside Walt Disney's Enchanted Tiki Room, guests can buy the treat in line for the show and eat it while listening to the "birds sing words and the flowers croon!"

SERVES 6

1 cup room-temperature water
1½ cups granulated sugar
2 cups chilled pineapple juice
1 tablespoon lime juice

1. In a medium microwave-safe bowl, combine water and sugar. Microwave 1 minute, stir, then microwave 1 more minute and stir to create a syrup. Cover and refrigerate at least 2 hours.

2. Pour pineapple juice into ice cream machine and add ½ cup chilled syrup. Add lime juice. Follow ice cream machine instructions and run about 20 minutes.

3. Serve immediately or transfer to a large plastic container, cover, and freeze overnight for a harder consistency.

DID YOU KNOW?

The "real" Dole Whip at Disneyland is prepared with a premade powder and water mixture. This recipe can be made at home without purchasing the mix and tastes just like the original!

Pineapple Upside Down Cake

Adventureland, Magic Kingdom

* * * ✦ * * *

This delicious cake is served at Aloha Isle, next to Walt Disney's Enchanted Tiki Room and across from The Magic Carpets of Aladdin attraction. In order to get the full experience, make Dole Whip (see recipe in this chapter) to place on top of the Pineapple Upside Down Cake. The combination of cold soft serve and sweet cake is not to be missed!

SERVES 18

½ cup salted butter, melted
1 cup light brown sugar
2 (20-ounce) cans pineapple rings packed in juice, drained (reserve juice)
1 (15.25-ounce) box yellow cake mix
3 large eggs
½ cup salted butter, softened

1. Preheat oven to 350°F. Grease three jumbo muffin tins with nonstick cooking spray and set aside.

2. In a small bowl, mix together melted butter and brown sugar until combined. Spoon about 2 tablespoons mixture into the bottom of each muffin cup.

3. Place 1 pineapple ring into eighteen muffin cups, reserving pineapple juice.

4. Pour reserved pineapple juice into a 1-cup measuring cup. Add water if necessary to make 1 cup. In the bowl of a stand mixer, add pineapple juice, dry cake mix, eggs, and softened butter. Using the flat beater attachment, beat on low speed 30 seconds, then on high speed 2 minutes.

5. Use a ⅓-cup measuring cup or cookie scoop to put batter into muffin cups on top of pineapple.

6. Bake until a knife inserted in center comes out clean, about 20 minutes. Let cool in pan at least 3 minutes before attempting to remove.

7. Use a butter knife to loosen the sides of the cakes. Place a clean baking sheet on the cakes and flip over, tipping the cakes out onto the baking sheet.

Maple Popcorn

Frontierland, Magic Kingdom

· · · · ✦ · · ·

Flavored popcorns have become all the rage at Disney Parks over the years. And like regular buttered popcorn, many of the flavored popcorns are also eligible for refills at Disney locations using the refillable popcorn buckets! This Maple Popcorn has a similar texture to caramel popcorn, but with a distinct smoky-sweet element that only maple can bring.

SERVES 15

1⅓ cups granulated sugar
1 cup cold salted butter
¼ cup pure maple syrup
¼ cup light corn syrup
½ teaspoon salt
1 teaspoon maple flavoring
1 teaspoon vanilla extract
20 cups popped popcorn

1. In a medium saucepan over medium heat, add sugar, butter, maple syrup, corn syrup, and salt. Cook and stir until butter is melted and ingredients are combined, about 3 minutes. Stir occasionally until temperature reaches 300°F. Remove from heat and add maple flavoring and vanilla extract.

2. Put about half of the popped popcorn into a large paper grocery bag. Carefully pour about half of the maple sauce over popcorn. Add remaining popcorn, then remaining maple sauce.

3. Roll down the top of bag and, wearing mitts or using hot pads, shake bag vigorously to coat all the popcorn. Carefully pour coated popcorn onto wax or parchment paper on countertop and use a rubber spatula to spread evenly and break up large chunks.

4. Let sit about 20 minutes to allow coating to harden. Store leftovers in an airtight container up to 1 week.

CHAPTER 5

EPCOT

EPCOT is the foodie center of Walt Disney World Resort. People literally travel to this park just to eat! Instead of the hub-and-spoke systems of Disneyland and Magic Kingdom, EPCOT has a central lake with "lands" circling it. Guests enter the park and are immediately met by the iconic geodesic sphere that is Spaceship Earth. Board a Friend-ship to the World Showcase and let your senses take over as you smell, and prepare to taste, morsels from around the world. Eleven countries are represented here, and most have at least one sit-down restaurant, a counter service restaurant, and multiple snack and treat outlets. In the words of the great food writer Andrew Zimmern, "If it looks good, eat it!" Of course, no travel is required, thanks to the recipes in this chapter. You can plan a special night around recipes from a specific country, or sample favorites from multiple places in one sitting!

★ 1 **CROISSANT DOUGHNUTS**
(Future World, EPCOT)

★ 2 **MACARON ICE CREAM SANDWICHES**
(France, EPCOT)

★ 3 **CROQUE GLACÉ**
(France, EPCOT)

★ 4 **NAPOLEONS**
(France, EPCOT)

★ 5 **CRÊPES**
(France, EPCOT)

★ 6 **TARTE AUX FRAISES**
(France, EPCOT)

★ 7 **SCHOOL BREAD**
(Norway, EPCOT)

★ 8 **TROLL HORNS**
(Norway, EPCOT)

★ 9 **CARAMEL POPCORN**
(Germany, EPCOT)

★ 10 **CHOCOLATE-CARAMEL PINEAPPLE SPEARS** (Germany, EPCOT)

★ 11 **CARAMEL PECAN BARS**
(Germany, EPCOT)

★ 12 **BAVARIAN CHEESECAKE**
(Germany, EPCOT)

★ 13 **STRAWBERRY KAKIGŌRI**
(Japan, EPCOT)

★ 14 **MELON KAKIGŌRI**
(Japan, EPCOT)

★ 15 **MANGO POPSICLES**
(Mexico, EPCOT)

★ 16 **COCONUT POPSICLES**
(Mexico, EPCOT)

★ 17 **COCCO GELATO**
(Italy, EPCOT)

★ 18 **STRACCIATELLA GELATO**
(Italy, EPCOT)

★ 19 **BAKLAVA**
(Morocco, EPCOT)

Croissant Doughnuts

Future World, EPCOT

You may know this delicious pastry better as a "Cronut," patented by the inventor, Dominique Ansel of New York City's Dominique Ansel Bakery, in 2013. Since then, many places have created a version of his doughnut, including Walt Disney World Resort. This treat used to be sold only at EPCOT festivals, but it was such a favorite that it became a full-time food item in Future World at Electric Umbrella. Now you can make it in your own home with this easy-to-follow recipe.

SERVES 8

3 cups vegetable oil for frying
1 (16.3-ounce) can refrigerated biscuit dough
½ cup granulated sugar
1 teaspoon ground cinnamon

1. In a large, heavy-bottomed pot over medium-high heat, add vegetable oil. It should measure to a depth of about 2". Heat until oil reaches 375°F.

2. Cut a 1" hole in center of each biscuit. Carefully slide 2 biscuits into the hot oil. Fry 1 minute per side.

3. Remove doughnuts to a cooling rack. Repeat with remaining doughnuts.

4. Mix together sugar and cinnamon in a medium shallow dish. Coat each doughnut in the cinnamon sugar.

Macaron Ice Cream Sandwiches

France, EPCOT

· · · ✦ · · ·

EPCOT matches its character meet-and-greets with characters' stories that originate from the countries in the World Showcase. Characters you can expect to see in the France pavilion include Belle and the Beast (from *Beauty and the Beast*); Aurora (from *Sleeping Beauty*); Marie, Berlioz, and Toulouse (from *The Aristocats*); and Remy (from *Ratatouille*). The combination of the crisp shells and the cold, creamy ice cream creates a party in your mouth: a perfect pairing for a Disney movie marathon indoors on a hot day, or your next warm-weather party.

YIELDS 6 MACARONS

12 (3"-wide) Raspberry Rose Mickey Macaron shells (see recipe in Chapter 3)

3 cups ice cream, any flavor

Place a scoop of ice cream between two shells. Repeat with remaining ice cream and shells. Enjoy immediately.

MIX IT UP

An easy way to switch up this recipe is to sub out for different flavors of ice cream. Vanilla variations provide a classic base that lets the macaron shells shine, while a busier flavor like Rocky Road or Mint Chocolate Chip allow the ice cream to be the star!

Croque Glacé

France, EPCOT

· · · · ✦ · · ·

At L'Artisan des Glaces shop at the France pavilion in EPCOT, these ice cream sandwiches are served custom-made. You can choose one of sixteen delicious flavors of ice cream, as well as strawberry or chocolate sauce. The French Cast Member will then slice in half a fresh brioche bun, scoop in your selection of ice cream, and drizzle on your choice of sauce. They then place the whole thing in a special press made just for this treat. It sticks the edges of the bread together and seals the ice cream into the center. Now you can have this heavenly treat right at home!

YIELDS 4 SANDWICHES

1 cup whole milk
¼ cup granulated sugar
2 teaspoons active dry yeast
4½ cups all-purpose flour
1 teaspoon salt
5 large eggs, divided
½ cup salted butter, softened
1 teaspoon room-temperature water
4 cups ice cream, any flavor
¼ cup chocolate sauce

1. Preheat oven to 350°F.

2. In a large microwave-safe bowl, microwave milk on high 30 seconds. Stir. Microwave an additional 30 seconds. Repeat until milk stabilizes at 110°F. Stir in sugar and yeast and allow to sit 15 minutes.

3. In the bowl of a stand mixer, add flour and salt. Add yeast mixture. Using the dough hook attachment, start mixing on low speed. Add 4 eggs, one at a time. Once most of the flour is incorporated, add butter 1 tablespoon at a time. Turn the speed up to high and knead about 10 minutes.

4. Shape dough into a ball and transfer to a large greased bowl. Cover with plastic wrap. Let rise in a warm place 1 hour.

5. Line an ungreased baking sheet with parchment paper and set aside.

(continued) ▶

6. Lightly flour a flat surface and turn the dough out onto the flour. Flatten dough slightly with your hand until dough is about 1" thick. Cut dough like a pizza into eight equal triangles. Form each piece into a ball by tucking dough underneath and pulling the top taut. Place all eight balls on prepared baking sheet, cover with plastic, and allow to rise 30 minutes.

7. In a small bowl, whisk remaining egg and water together. Brush generously over buns. Bake 25 minutes or until tops are golden brown. Cool slightly on a cooling rack, about 10 minutes.

8. Slice buns in half. Carefully remove bread from the middle of the buns (or press down with your fingers if you like a denser sandwich). Scoop a baseball-sized portion of ice cream into the center of 4 buns. Drizzle with chocolate sauce. Press buns together. Repeat to make 4 sandwiches.

DID YOU KNOW?

Brioche Ice Cream sandwiches, although sold at the France pavilion at EPCOT, are actually an Italian invention. Sicilians created this sweet treat, which has since spread across most of Europe. No one can resist this delicious combination!

Napoleons

France, EPCOT

Another name for this French dessert is *mille-feuille*, which translates to "one thousand leaves" or "one thousand layers." Although you can only see three pastry layers and two crème layers, there are in fact countless layers! Puff pastry is made by flattening pastry, laying down a sheet of butter, and folding. This is then chilled and repeated over and over, until the folds create hundreds of layers. The following recipe makes things easier by using prepared frozen puff pastry.

SERVES 6

1 (17.3-ounce) box frozen puff pastry sheets
1 tablespoon granulated sugar
1½ cups Crème Pâtissière (see Tarte aux Fraises recipe in this chapter)
1 cup confectioners' sugar, divided
2 tablespoons whole milk, divided
1 teaspoon cocoa powder

1. Allow puff pastry to thaw at room temperature 40 minutes.

2. Preheat oven to 400°F. Line an ungreased baking sheet with parchment paper.

3. Lay puff pastry flat on prepared baking sheet. Use a fork to poke holes across entire surface of pastry.

4. Sprinkle pastry with sugar. Lay a sheet of parchment paper on top of pastry, then a layer of aluminum foil. Place another baking sheet on top of the foil to keep the pastry from puffing up. Bake 15 minutes.

5. Remove extra baking sheet, foil, and top parchment paper. Bake 8 more minutes. Flip pastry and bake an additional 7 minutes, or until golden brown and crisp.

6. Transfer pastry to a cooling rack to cool completely, about 1 hour.

7. Once pastry is completely cool, cut off crispy edges, then cut into eighteen rectangles, approximately 2" × 4".

8. Set aside six of the rectangles.

(continued) ▶

9. Working with the remaining twelve rectangles, for each pastry, lay down one rectangle on a flat surface and spread about 2 tablespoons Crème Pâtissière on top. Add another layer of pastry followed by another layer of Crème Pâtissière. Repeat to create six pastries.

10. In a small bowl, stir together ½ cup confectioners' sugar and 1 tablespoon milk to create a thin icing.

11. In a separate small bowl, mix remaining ½ cup confectioners' sugar, remaining 1 tablespoon milk, and cocoa powder to make chocolate icing. Transfer to a piping bag or small plastic bag with a corner snipped off.

12. To finish each Napoleon, use a knife to spread the white icing onto one of the reserved pastry rectangles. Pipe four or five diagonal lines of chocolate icing across the length of the rectangle on top of the still-wet white icing. Drag a toothpick in three perpendicular diagonal lines across the first three lines of chocolate, making all strokes toward yourself, creating a crosshatch pattern. Drag the toothpick between each of the last three diagonal lines, making all strokes away from yourself. Place this decorated pastry on top of the other layers. Repeat layering and icing decorations with remaining pastry rectangles and Crème Pâtissière.

Crêpes

France, EPCOT

· · · · ✦ · · ·

EPCOT serves Crêpes five ways: butter and sugar, strawberry preserves, chocolate, chocolate-hazelnut, or à la mode (with ice cream). You can make any of these variations at home using the following recipe as a base. You can even go totally crazy and come up with new toppings that EPCOT doesn't sell! How about bananas? Or ham and cheese? Crêpes are a wonderfully simple vessel that taste delicious with almost anything.

SERVES 6

1 cup all-purpose flour
2 cups whole milk
4 large egg whites
1 tablespoon vegetable oil
1 tablespoon amber honey
½ teaspoon salt

1. In a blender, add all ingredients and blend until well combined, about 30 seconds.

2. Heat a large nonstick frying pan over medium heat 30 seconds. Coat pan with nonstick cooking spray. Pour about ¼ cup batter directly from the blender into the center of the pan, swirling while pouring, to fill the pan with a thin layer of batter.

3. Allow to cook about 1½ minutes. Once the edges are brown and pulling away from the sides, slide a rubber spatula around the entire edge of the batter, slip spatula under the Crêpe, and flip. Cook an additional 1½ minutes on the other side. Remove to a large plate.

4. Repeat with remaining batter, spraying the pan between each Crêpe.

5. Lay out a Crêpe and fill with whatever toppings you desire, then fold in half, then in thirds. Repeat with remaining Crêpes.

DID YOU KNOW?

The word crêpe *comes from the Latin* crispus, *meaning "curled." However, crêpes are known to be served in many different shapes, such as half-moons, triangles, rolled, or folded into packets.*

Tarte aux Fraises

France, EPCOT

· · · · ✦ · · ·

This delicious French favorite can be made faster with a few easy substitutions. Instead of making homemade shells, buy tart shells from the grocery store baking aisle. Instead of making Crème Pâtissière, whip up a (3.4-ounce) package of instant vanilla pudding, using 1½ cups milk instead of 2 cups. The result will have a similar flavor profile with an easier execution.

SERVES 8

For Tarte Shells

1¼ cups all-purpose flour
½ cup confectioners' sugar
¼ teaspoon salt
½ cup cold salted butter, cut into ¼" cubes
1 large egg
½ teaspoon vanilla extract

1. In a food processor, add flour, confectioners' sugar, and salt. Pulse five times to mix. Add butter cubes gradually, pulsing five times between each addition, until mixture resembles coarse crumbs. Add egg and vanilla and pulse a few more times, until the dough pulls together into a rough ball.

2. Remove dough from food processor and place on a sheet of plastic wrap. Wrap and flatten into a disk ½" thick. Refrigerate 1 hour.

For Crème Pâtissière

2 cups whole milk
6 tablespoons granulated sugar
3 large egg yolks
1 large egg
2½ tablespoons cornstarch
¼ teaspoon salt
1 tablespoon vanilla extract
3 tablespoons cold salted butter

1. In a medium saucepan over medium heat, heat milk, stirring frequently. Once the milk just starts to bubble around the edges of the pan, about 2 minutes, remove from heat. Set aside.

2. In the bowl of a stand mixer, add sugar, egg yolks, whole egg, cornstarch, salt, and vanilla. Using the whisk attachment, beat until well combined.

(continued) ▶

124

3. While continuing to beat, pour ½ cup warm milk slowly into egg mixture. Add another ½ cup milk while still beating.

4. Pour egg mixture into saucepan with remaining milk. Over medium heat, whisk by hand 2 minutes until custard starts to thicken. Lower heat to a simmer and continue to whisk 2 more minutes.

5. Remove custard from heat and whisk in butter 1 tablespoon at a time until melted. Pour custard through a sieve into a large bowl and cover immediately with plastic wrap. Ensure plastic wrap is tight against the surface of the custard. Refrigerate 2 hours.

6. Preheat oven to 375°F. Grease a jumbo muffin tin with nonstick cooking spray and set aside.

7. Remove dough from refrigerator and roll out to ¼" thickness on a flour-covered surface. Use a circular cookie cutter or lid about 4" in diameter to cut out circles of dough.

8. Press dough circles snugly into muffin cups. Cut squares of aluminum foil and press foil gently into the dough in each muffin cup. Fill each cup with dried beans or uncooked rice. Bake 15 minutes.

9. Remove from oven and allow to cool 15 minutes then remove beans or rice and foil and allow shells to cool completely, at least 30 minutes, before filling.

For Topping

- 1 cup fresh strawberries, hulled and sliced
- 1 tablespoon granulated sugar

1. Lay sliced strawberries on a medium plate. Sprinkle with sugar. Set aside.

2. Scoop Crème Pâtissière into a pastry bag fitted with a large star tip. Pipe Crème Pâtissière into each shell, swirling up to a point. Lay strawberry slices around the sides. Top each Crème Pâtissière swirl with 1 strawberry slice.

School Bread

Norway, EPCOT

· · · ✦ · · ·

School Bread, or skoleboller, is a typical Norwegian treat. Its name comes from the fact that schoolchildren often take it in their lunches, and it is typically served at school functions. Every bakery in Norway offers fresh Skoleboller. The combination of springy spiced dough, cold custard filling, and flaky coconut on top delights Norwegians and Walt Disney World guests alike.

SERVES 8

- 3 tablespoons salted butter, melted
- 2 cups warm water (110°F)
- 5 cups all-purpose flour
- 4 tablespoons granulated sugar
- ½ teaspoon ground cinnamon
- 4 tablespoons active dry yeast
- 1 cup confectioners' sugar
- 3 tablespoons heavy cream
- 1 teaspoon vanilla extract
- 1 (3.4-ounce) box instant vanilla pudding
- 1½ cups whole milk
- 1 cup sweetened shredded coconut

1. Grease a large bowl with nonstick cooking spray. Set aside.

2. In the bowl of a stand mixer, add butter, water, flour, granulated sugar, cinnamon, and yeast. Using the dough hook attachment, knead 5 minutes. Then place in greased bowl. Cover with plastic wrap and let rise in a warm place 30 minutes.

3. Preheat oven to 375°F. Line an ungreased baking sheet with parchment paper and set aside.

4. Turn dough out onto lightly floured surface and cut into eight equal pieces. Form each piece into a ball by tucking excess dough under and creating a taut top. Place on prepared baking sheet, evenly spaced apart, and allow to rise an additional 5 minutes.

5. Bake dough 12 minutes, until golden brown. Let cool on baking sheet 10 minutes.

6. In a small shallow bowl, stir together confectioners' sugar and cream. Set aside. In a separate medium bowl, whisk together vanilla, instant pudding powder, and milk. Chill pudding mixture 5 minutes, then spoon into a piping bag fitted with any size tip. Pour coconut into another shallow bowl and set aside.

7. To assemble: Cut a 1" hole out of the top of each bun. Pull out or push down bread inside bun. Invert bun and dip whole top side into the cream mixture. Then immediately roll in coconut. Pipe pudding into the hole and fill inside of bun, ending with a small swirl on top of bun.

Troll Horns

Norway, EPCOT

· · · · ✦ · · ·

Opened in 1988, the Norway pavilion is the newest country in the World Showcase. The then Crown Prince Harald V of Norway led the dedication ceremony himself, and he even broadcast the ceremony all the way to (the real) Norway. Trolls are an essential part of Norse mythology, hence the Troll Horn! This horn is made from flaky puff pastry and is the perfect balance to the sweet cream inside.

SERVES 6

For Horns

1 (17.3-ounce) box frozen puff pastry sheets
1 tablespoon vegetable oil
1 large egg
1 tablespoon room-temperature water

1. Allow puff pastry to thaw at room temperature 40 minutes. Preheat oven to 400°F. Line an ungreased baking sheet with parchment paper and set aside.

2. Construct six cones by rolling a piece of 8" × 11" parchment paper into a cone shape, and sealing completely with tape. Wrap outside of cone smoothly in aluminum foil. Brush foil with oil.

3. Lay out puff pastry sheets. Use a pizza cutter or knife to cut into strips ½" wide. In a small bowl, whisk together egg and water. Briefly dip each strip in egg wash.

4. Starting at the bottom of a cone, wrap strips of pastry up the cone, pulling the pastry tightly and slightly overlapping each layer. Repeat with remaining cones.

5. Place pastry-covered cones on prepared baking sheet. Bake until golden brown, about 15 minutes. Remove from oven and allow to cool completely, about 30 minutes, on baking sheet. Remove cones from pastry, retaining cone shape.

For Orange Cream

½ cup heavy cream

2 ounces cream cheese, softened

2 tablespoons confectioners' sugar

1 tablespoon orange marmalade

½ cup granulated sugar

2 tablespoons salted butter, melted

1. In the bowl of a stand mixer, add heavy cream, cream cheese, and confectioners' sugar. Using the whisk attachment, beat on high speed until stiff peaks form. Add orange marmalade and stir until combined. Spoon cream into a large piping bag fitted with a large star tip.

2. Place granulated sugar in a shallow dish. Once cones are cooled, brush with melted butter and roll in sugar. Place tip of piping bag into bottom of a cone, filling from bottom to top. Repeat with remaining cones. Serve.

MIX IT UP

An easy change-up for this recipe: Use a different marmalade or jam flavor instead of orange. Give classic strawberry or grape a try! This small change delivers a yummy flavor variation.

Caramel Popcorn

Germany, EPCOT

· · · · ✦ · · ·

Although lots of popcorn flavors are available around the Walt Disney World Resort, this recipe stands out as a fan favorite. Confectioners can be seen making Caramel Popcorn fresh at the Karamell-Küche in the Germany pavilion. Who could resist the delicious smell and the promise of that amazing crunch?

SERVES 6

½ cup cold salted butter
1 cup light brown sugar
¼ cup light corn syrup
½ teaspoon salt
¼ teaspoon baking soda
½ teaspoon vanilla extract
10 cups popped popcorn

1. Preheat oven to 250°F. Line a large ungreased baking sheet with parchment paper and set aside.

2. In a medium saucepan over medium heat, stir together butter, brown sugar, corn syrup, and salt. Bring to a boil. Once boiling, let cook 4 minutes without stirring. Remove from heat. Quickly stir in baking soda and vanilla.

3. Pour half of the popped popcorn into a large paper bag. Pour half the caramel sauce onto the popcorn. Add remaining popcorn, then remaining sauce. Fold down the top of the bag and, using hot pads, shake the bag vigorously 30 seconds to coat popcorn thoroughly.

4. Pour coated popcorn onto prepared baking sheet. Flatten popcorn into a single layer. Bake 1 hour, stirring every 15 minutes.

5. Remove from oven and stir one last time. Allow to cool completely, about 30 minutes. Store in an airtight bag at room temperature up to 3 days.

Chocolate-Caramel Pineapple Spears

Germany, EPCOT

. . . ✦ . . .

These pineapple spears are sold at the Karamell-Küche shop in the Germany pavilion at EPCOT. In fact, Karamell-Küche is operated by the Werther's company and is the only freestanding Werther's store on the planet. Next time you eat one of those delicious hard candies from the grocery store, you can dream about Karamell-Küche, where many treats are coated in the stuff. Yum!

SERVES 8

1 large fresh pineapple, peeled, cored, and sliced into 8 spears
1 cup semisweet chocolate chips
1 cup Werther's Original Soft Caramels, unwrapped
1 tablespoon whole milk

1. Grease a large plate with nonstick cooking spray and set aside.

2. Lay pineapple spears on several sheets of paper towels. Add a paper towel or clean dishcloth over the top and gently blot to remove moisture. Let sit while you proceed with the next steps.

3. In a medium microwave-safe bowl, add chocolate chips. Microwave on high 30 seconds, stir, then microwave 15 seconds. Repeat microwaving in 15-second increments, stirring between each, until chocolate just barely melts. Dip each spear into the chocolate (you can use a spoon to help it along), then place dipped spears on greased plate. Chill in the refrigerator 30 minutes.

4. In a separate medium microwave-safe bowl, add caramels and milk. Microwave on high 30 seconds, stir, then microwave 15 seconds. Repeat microwaving in 15-second increments, stirring between each, until caramel just barely melts. Remove spears from the refrigerator and drizzle caramel over spears. Chill in refrigerator another 30 minutes before serving.

Caramel Pecan Bars

Germany, EPCOT

· · · · ✦ · · · ·

When the Germany pavilion at EPCOT was first dreamed up in the late 1970s, Germany itself was split into two nations: East and West. Imagineers wanted the pavilion to focus not on the division but instead their shared heritage. The original pavilion was also supposed to have a ride that would take guests on a cruise down the Rhine River. The ride never came to fruition, but you can now take an Adventures by Disney river cruise on the *actual* Rhine River! Created from the German Werther's candy, this recipe is delicious as is, but if you'd like, sub the pecans for walnuts, almonds, or M&M's.

YIELDS 12 BARS

1 cup salted butter, softened
½ cup granulated sugar
¼ teaspoon salt
2 cups all-purpose flour
1 (4.51-ounce) bag Werther's Original Soft Caramels, unwrapped
1 (14-ounce) can sweetened condensed milk
½ cup chopped pecans
½ teaspoon vanilla extract

1. Preheat oven to 350°F. Line an ungreased 9" × 13" baking dish with parchment paper and set aside.

2. In the bowl of a stand mixer, add butter, sugar, and salt. Using the flat beater attachment, cream together well. Add flour slowly and mix until well combined. Press two-thirds of dough into the prepared baking dish, reserving the remaining dough.

3. In a medium microwave-safe bowl, add caramels and milk. Microwave on high for 1½ minutes. Stir and microwave an additional 1 minute until caramels are melted. Stir in pecans and vanilla.

4. Pour caramel sauce over dough in pan. Scatter flattened pieces, about 1" in diameter each, of remaining dough across the top.

5. Bake until edges are bubbling and golden brown, about 25 minutes. Allow to cool completely, about 1 hour, before cutting into bars. Cover and store in the refrigerator up to 7 days.

Bavarian Cheesecake

Germany, EPCOT

· · · · ✦ · · · ·

The Bavarian Cheesecake is served at the Biergarten Restaurant in the Germany pavilion of EPCOT. This restaurant definitely has a unique atmosphere: Black paint on the ceiling simulates a night sky, bringing the magic of a German outdoor festival to life—indoors, in central Florida! This decadently creamy cheesecake is served in enormous portions. Give it a unique twist by topping with sliced strawberries or drizzling each slice with chocolate sauce.

SERVES 6

For Sponge Cakes

¾ cup granulated sugar
4 large egg yolks
1 teaspoon vanilla extract
¾ cup all-purpose flour
1 teaspoon baking powder
½ teaspoon salt
4 large egg whites

1. Preheat oven to 375°F. Line two ungreased 9" cake pans with parchment paper disks cut to fit. Grease the sides of each pan with nonstick cooking spray and set aside.

2. In the bowl of a stand mixer, add sugar, egg yolks, and vanilla. Using the flat beater attachment, beat on high until thick and pale colored, about 3 minutes. Gradually add flour (¼ cup at a time), baking powder, and salt, beating until smooth.

3. In a clean bowl of a stand mixer, add egg whites. Using the whisk attachment, beat on high until soft peaks form, about 5 minutes. Carefully fold egg whites into flour mixture.

4. Divide batter equally between prepared cake pans. Bake until a toothpick inserted comes out clean, about 10 minutes. Set pans aside to let cakes cool completely, about 1 hour.

5. Line an ungreased 9" springform cake pan with parchment paper disk cut to fit. Set aside.

For Cream Cheese Filling

1 (¼-ounce) packet
  unflavored gelatin
4 tablespoons warm water
1½ cups heavy cream
12 ounces cream cheese,
  softened
2 large egg yolks
½ cup granulated sugar
1 cup sour cream
2 tablespoons lemon juice

1. In a small bowl, dissolve gelatin in water. Set aside.

2. In the bowl of a stand mixer, add heavy cream. Using the whisk attachment, beat on high until soft peaks form, about 3 minutes; set aside.

3. In a separate clean bowl of a stand mixer, add cream cheese, egg yolks, sugar, sour cream, and lemon juice. Using the whisk attachment, beat on high until smooth. Gently fold in whipped cream. Add gelatin mixture to bowl and stir until well combined.

For Topping

2 tablespoons confectioners'
  sugar

Remove cakes from cake pans by running a butter knife along the edges and carefully inverting to release the cake. Place one Sponge Cake snugly into the bottom of prepared springform pan. Spoon Cream Cheese Filling on top of cake and spread evenly. Top with remaining Sponge Cake. Allow to chill covered in the refrigerator 6 hours or overnight. To remove from the springform pan, release the clasp and slide off the side ring. Sift confectioners' sugar over the top before serving.

Strawberry Kakigōri

Japan, EPCOT

· · · · ✦ · · · ·

This delicious treat has reportedly been around since the eleventh century. Back then, ice was not crushed by a fancy machine; it was thinly shaved off a massive block using a huge sword. Talk about presentation! Nowadays, Kakigōri are very similar to Western-style snow cones and have similar popular flavors like cherry, raspberry, and "Hawaiian Blue." Nothing refreshes quite like a shaved ice treat on a hot summer day.

SERVES 6

1 pound unsweetened frozen strawberries
1 cup granulated sugar
1 tablespoon lemon juice
6 cups shaved ice
¾ cup canned sweetened condensed milk

1. In a medium saucepan over medium heat, add strawberries, sugar, and lemon juice. Bring to a boil and cook 3 minutes, stirring frequently, until bubbly. Do not mash strawberries. After 3 minutes, strain juice into a medium bowl. Discard solids. Chill covered in the refrigerator at least 3 hours.

2. Fill six serving bowls with shaved ice. Pour strawberry syrup over ice. Drizzle 2 tablespoons sweetened condensed milk over each serving.

Melon Kakigōri

Japan, EPCOT

· · · ✦ · · ·

One of the best ways to experience the Japan pavilion at EPCOT is to pick up a cold kakigōri (shaved ice) treat and listen to the Matsuriza troupe play the taiko drums. These massive drums are held under the central pagoda and deliver a powerful rhythmic sound. You can re-create the experience at home when you make this recipe by playing a video of the drums online as you stir!

SERVES 6

½ large cantaloupe, peeled, seeded, and diced
1 cup granulated sugar
1 tablespoon lemon juice
6 cups shaved ice
¾ cup canned sweetened condensed milk

1. In a medium saucepan over medium heat, add cantaloupe, sugar, and lemon juice. Bring to a boil and cook 3 minutes, stirring frequently. Do not mash cantaloupe. After 3 minutes, strain juice into a medium bowl. Discard solids. Chill covered in the refrigerator at least 3 hours.

2. Fill six serving bowls with shaved ice. Pour melon syrup over ice. Drizzle 2 tablespoons sweetened condensed milk over each serving.

Mango Popsicles

Mexico, EPCOT

· · · ✦ · · ·

Found by the Mexico pavilion courtyard, these fruity pops are the perfect treat to enjoy while catching a performance by Mariachi Cobre. This group was formed more than fifty years ago and graces Walt Disney World audiences with traditional favorites as well as songs from the hit Pixar film *Coco*. Bring a little tradition to your own kitchen with this simple recipe.

SERVES 8

1 cup plain vanilla yogurt
1 cup frozen mango chunks
½ cup granulated sugar

1. In a blender, combine all ingredients and blend until smooth. Leave some small chunks remaining if preferred.

2. Carefully pour mixture into Popsicle molds. Insert a wooden Popsicle stick upright into each mold. Allow to freeze solid overnight.

MIX IT UP

If you like your Popsicles with a little more substance, add more mango chunks to the Popsicle mold as you fill it. You can even get wild and add shredded coconut to the Mango Popsicles for a delicious blend of different fruity flavors.

Coconut Popsicles

Mexico, EPCOT

· · · ✳ · · ·

These sweet Coconut Popsicles really hit the spot on a hot day. EPCOT is the hottest of all the Disney Parks in Florida because it has the most cement and the least tree coverage. The walkway around the World Showcase is a whopping 1.2 miles long, so make sure you're taking time out for refreshments! These treats are available at La Cantina de San Ángel or sometimes in mobile freezer carts around the Mexico pavilion.

SERVES 8

1 (13.5-ounce) can coconut milk
½ cup whole milk
½ cup heavy cream
½ cup granulated sugar

1. In a large microwave-safe bowl, combine all ingredients. Microwave on high 30 seconds. Stir. Microwave an additional 30 seconds. Stir.

2. Carefully pour mixture into Popsicle molds. Insert a wooden Popsicle stick upright into each mold. Allow to freeze solid overnight.

Cocco Gelato

Italy, EPCOT

· · · · ✦ · · · ·

Cocco Gelato is a creamy Italian coconut ice cream, typically served in small portions and often with a little shovel-like spoon. It is the perfect food to eat while strolling around the Italian pavilion at EPCOT. Now, Italy is even closer to home with this simple recipe! Whip up a big batch to enjoy over the next week, or share a bowl with a loved one as you look through photos of the Italian pavilion.

SERVES 6

3 cups unsweetened shredded coconut, divided
2 cups whole milk
2 teaspoons vanilla extract
1 cup granulated sugar
¼ teaspoon salt
5 large egg yolks, beaten
1 (13.5-ounce) can coconut milk
1 cup heavy cream

1. Set oven to broil on high. Line an ungreased baking sheet with parchment paper and set aside.

2. Lay shredded coconut in a single layer on lined baking sheet. Broil 12 minutes, checking and stirring every 5 minutes, until coconut is a toasty golden brown. Remove toasted coconut to a medium bowl.

3. In a medium saucepan over medium heat, combine whole milk, vanilla, sugar, salt, and 2½ cups toasted coconut. Once mixture starts to bubble, remove from heat.

4. Use an immersion blender (or use a regular blender) to blend until mixture is smooth. Pour through a sieve, discarding solids, and return to saucepan over medium heat.

5. In a medium bowl, add beaten egg yolks. Use a ladle to slowly pour a small stream of the milk mixture into bowl while whisking continuously. Continue until half the milk mixture has been added.

6. Carefully and slowly pour the yolk mixture into remaining milk mixture in saucepan, continuing to whisk. Whisk continuously about 5 minutes while custard thickens, then remove from heat.

(continued) ▶

7. Pour mixture through a sieve again to remove any egg solids. Stir in coconut milk and cream. Refrigerate covered 1 hour.

8. When chilled, pour into an ice cream machine. Follow manufacturer's instructions and run 15 minutes. Add ¼ cup toasted coconut, then run an additional 5 minutes.

9. Scoop into a large plastic container or a loaf pan lined with parchment paper. Sprinkle remaining ¼ cup toasted coconut over top. Cover and freeze until solid, about 4 hours.

MIX IT UP

Coconut flakes in ice cream not your thing? At the end of this recipe, just omit adding the final ¼ cup toasted coconut into the mix. And if you decide you'd like just a little, sprinkle some onto your individual serving!

Stracciatella Gelato

Italy, EPCOT

The word *stracciatella* is used to describe three food items in Italy: a cheese made from Italian buffalo milk, a soup made with dropped eggs, and an ice cream with chocolate pieces in it. The ice cream was actually called *stracciatella* after the soup, since the creator thought the chocolate pieces looked like the egg pieces in the soup. The gelato shop in EPCOT only serves the ice cream, so you're in the clear from accidentally ordering soup or cheese!

SERVES 6

2 cups whole milk
1 cup heavy cream
⅔ cup granulated sugar
1 tablespoon light corn syrup
1 tablespoon vanilla extract
¼ teaspoon salt
3 large egg yolks, beaten
½ cup finely chopped dark chocolate chips, divided

1. In a medium saucepan over medium heat, combine milk, cream, sugar, corn syrup, vanilla, and salt. Once mixture starts to bubble, remove from heat.

2. In a medium bowl, add beaten egg yolks. Use a ladle to slowly pour a small stream of milk mixture into bowl while whisking continuously. Continue until half the milk mixture has been added.

3. Return saucepan to medium heat. Carefully and slowly pour yolk mixture into remaining milk mixture in saucepan, continuing to whisk. Whisk continuously about 5 minutes while custard thickens, then remove from heat.

4. Pour mixture through a sieve to remove any egg solids. Refrigerate covered 1 hour.

5. When chilled, pour into an ice cream machine. Follow manufacturer's instructions and run 15 minutes Add ¼ cup chopped dark chocolate chips, then run an additional 5 minutes.

6. Scoop gelato into a large plastic container or loaf pan lined with parchment paper. Sprinkle remaining ¼ cup dark chocolate chips over top. Cover and freeze until solid, about 4 hours.

Baklava

Morocco, EPCOT

Although Baklava is served in the Morocco pavilion at EPCOT, its roots come from Turkey. In fact, Baklava, the ancestor of streusel, migrated to Hungary from Turkey in the sixteenth century. The Moroccan pavilion is known for its authenticity, as it was the only EPCOT pavilion to have that country's government assist in the design. This crispy, gooey, nutty pastry will transport you to the Moroccan pavilion time and again!

SERVES 15

¾ cup confectioners' sugar
1½ cups whole shelled walnuts
½ tablespoon ground cinnamon
15 sheets frozen phyllo dough, thawed
½ cup salted butter, melted
1 cup granulated sugar
½ cup room-temperature water
¼ cup amber honey

1. Preheat oven to 375°F.

2. In a food processor, combine confectioners' sugar, walnuts, and cinnamon. Process until consistency is like pebbles. Set aside.

3. Lay down one sheet of phyllo dough on a clean surface. Brush entire surface of dough with butter. Lay down a second sheet of dough on top of first sheet. Brush entire surface with about one-third of the butter. Lay down a third sheet of dough on top of second sheet. Brush entire surface with remaining butter.

4. Sprinkle about one-fifth walnut filling over dough. Roll the dough layers up like a tight jelly roll and place in an ungreased 9" × 13" baking pan. Repeat layering and rolling with remaining dough and filling until you have five rolls. Drizzle any leftover butter on top of the rolls.

5. Bake rolls until golden brown on top, about 25 minutes.

6. In a small saucepan over medium heat, combine granulated sugar and water. Bring to a boil. Allow to boil 3 minutes, stirring frequently. Remove from heat and stir in honey.

7. Pour honey mixture over still-hot dough rolls. Allow to sit at room temperature at least 1 hour.

8. Remove rolls from pan one at a time and slice each roll into three pieces on a diagonal. Baklava will keep up to 3 days when covered tightly and stored in the refrigerator.

CHAPTER 6

Disney's Hollywood Studios

Lights! Camera! Action! At Disney's Hollywood Studios, *you* get to be the star. "Citizens of Hollywood" greet you before you even enter the gates. But the best snacks and treats available here are found in the back of the park, in Star Wars: Galaxy's Edge and Toy Story Land. Bubbles full of mysterious liquid meet you as you cross into the spaceport of Batuu at the Milk Stand. Grab samples of Blue and Green Milk to see which flavor you savor. And once you're done defeating the First Order, you can shrink down to the size of a toy in Toy Story Land. Woody's Lunch Box offers delicious fare, like seasonally flavored Lunch Box Tarts. But don't wait until your next vacation to get in on the action. Thanks to the recipes in this chapter, you can shine the spotlight on your own kitchen whenever you please! Whip up some Perfect Popcorn for movie night, or some Mickey Pretzels to impress your friends.

⭐ 1 **CANDY APPLES** (Sunset Boulevard, Disney's Hollywood Studios)

⭐ 2 **PERFECT POPCORN** (Sunset Boulevard, Disney's Hollywood Studios)

⭐ 3 **CARROT CAKE COOKIES** (Hollywood Boulevard, Disney's Hollywood Studios)

⭐ 4 **BUTTERFINGER CUPCAKES** (Hollywood Boulevard, Disney's Hollywood Studios)

⭐ 5 **PRETZELS WITH CREAM CHEESE FILLING** (An Incredible Celebration, Disney's Hollywood Studios)

⭐ 6 **MICKEY PRETZELS** (An Incredible Celebration, Disney's Hollywood Studios)

⭐ 7 **CHOCOLATE-HAZELNUT LUNCH BOX TARTS** (Toy Story Land, Disney's Hollywood Studios)

⭐ 8 **LEMON-BLUEBERRY LUNCH BOX TARTS** (Toy Story Land, Disney's Hollywood Studios)

⭐ 9 **GREEN MILK** (Star Wars: Galaxy's Edge, Disney's Hollywood Studios)

⭐ 10 **BLUE MILK** (Star Wars: Galaxy's Edge, Disney's Hollywood Studios)

⭐ 11 **OUTPOST POPCORN MIX** (Star Wars: Galaxy's Edge, Disney's Hollywood Studios)

⭐ 12 **RONTO WRAPS** (Star Wars: Galaxy's Edge, Disney's Hollywood Studios)

⭐ 13 **PEANUT BUTTER AND JELLY MILK SHAKES** (Echo Lake, Disney's Hollywood Studios)

⭐ 14 **FROZEN CHOCOLATE-COVERED BANANAS** (Echo Lake, Disney's Hollywood Studios)

Candy Apples

Sunset Boulevard, Disney's Hollywood Studios

· · · ✦ · · ·

The Candy Apple was first invented in 1908 by confectioner William W. Kolb. Since then, eating a Candy Apple evokes a feeling of nostalgia mirrored in Disney's Hollywood Studios. Travel back to the golden age of Hollywood with this simple recipe and a favorite film.

SERVES 10

10 large Granny Smith apples
2 cups granulated sugar
1 cup light corn syrup
1½ cups room-temperature water
3 drops red gel food coloring

1. Lay a large sheet of parchment paper on a flat surface. Grease with nonstick cooking spray, then set aside.

2. Carefully push a Popsicle stick deep into the stem area of each apple. Set aside.

3. In a medium saucepan over medium heat, add sugar, corn syrup, and water. Stir until temperature reaches 300°F, about 5 minutes. Remove pan from heat and stir in red food coloring.

4. Dip each apple into the candy mixture to coat, then place on the parchment paper. Let sit 10 minutes to harden before serving.

Perfect Popcorn

Sunset Boulevard, Disney's Hollywood Studios

· · · ✦ · · ·

There are 324,000 pounds of popcorn, or 5.3 million bags, served *every year* at the Walt Disney World Resort. In fact, popcorn was one of the opening day refreshments served in 1955 at the Disneyland Resort. Walt Disney himself did a TV spot eating a delicious box of Main Street Popcorn. Popcorn is a perfect fit for Sunset Boulevard at Disney's Hollywood Studios, as we all know it's the best snack to munch on at the movies!

SERVES 6

1 tablespoon coconut oil
½ cup unpopped popcorn kernels
¾ teaspoon Flavacol, divided

1. In a large pot over medium heat, melt coconut oil. Add popcorn kernels and ½ teaspoon Flavacol. Stir, then cover pot.

2. Once kernels begin popping, about 4 minutes, wear oven mitts while carefully holding the lid on the pot and swirling the pot continuously. When popping slows, remove from heat.

3. Pour popcorn into a large bowl and sprinkle with remaining ¼ teaspoon Flavacol.

Carrot Cake Cookies

Hollywood Boulevard, Disney's Hollywood Studios

· · · · ✦ · · ·

Carrot Cake Cookies have been served at Disney's Hollywood Studios for a *very* long time but recently underwent a revamp with larger cookies and less frosting. When you make these at home, you can choose how much frosting you want to include!

YIELDS 6 COOKIES

For Cookies

½ cup salted butter, softened

½ cup light brown sugar

½ cup granulated sugar

1 large egg

1 teaspoon vanilla extract

1¼ cups all-purpose flour

½ teaspoon baking powder

½ teaspoon baking soda

1 teaspoon ground cinnamon

½ teaspoon salt

½ cup old-fashioned rolled oats

½ cup unsweetened shredded coconut

½ cup chopped walnuts

2 large carrots, peeled and shredded

1. Preheat oven to 350°F. Line two ungreased baking sheets with parchment paper and set aside.

2. In the bowl of a stand mixer, add butter, brown sugar, and granulated sugar. Using the flat beater attachment, cream together well. Add egg and vanilla. Beat until combined. Sprinkle in flour ¼ cup at a time while mixing. Add in baking powder, baking soda, cinnamon, and salt. Beat until combined.

3. In a food processor or blender, add oats, coconut, and walnuts. Process until consistency of coarse crumbs. Add mixture to stand mixer. Mix and set aside.

4. Add shredded carrots to dough and mix well.

5. Using a ⅓-cup cookie scoop, scoop dough into twelve balls onto prepared baking sheets, about 1" apart. Bake until sides begin to brown, about 12 minutes. Remove from oven and allow to cool completely, about 30 minutes.

For Cream Cheese Frosting

½ cup salted butter, softened

4 cups confectioners' sugar

8 ounces cream cheese, softened

2 tablespoons heavy cream

1. In a medium bowl, whisk all frosting ingredients together.

2. Spread Cream Cheese Frosting, or pipe with a piping bag, onto half the cookies. Place remaining cookies on top to create sandwiches. Store in an airtight container in the refrigerator up to 3 days.

Butterfinger Cupcakes

Hollywood Boulevard, Disney's Hollywood Studios

· · · · ✦ · · · ·

Butterfinger Cupcakes used to be sold at Starring Rolls Café at Disney's Hollywood Studios, but Starring Rolls Café was closed in 2017. When the Butterfinger Cupcakes were seen again at The Trolley Car Café, they were smaller than they were back at Starring Rolls. Apparently, they were re-created this way because they were too "top heavy" in the pastry case and were prone to falling over. Have no fear: These cupcakes follow the original huge design, so you can live on the edge.

YIELDS 6 CUPCAKES

For Cupcakes

Batter for Cookies and Cream Mickey Cupcakes (see recipe in Chapter 3)
½ cup fudge sauce

1. Preheat oven to 350°F. Line a jumbo muffin tin with jumbo cupcake liners. Divide Cupcake batter evenly among cups, filling cups three-quarters full. Bake until a toothpick stuck in the middle of one comes out clean, about 22 minutes. Remove Cupcakes from tin and allow to cool completely on a cooling rack, about 2 hours.

2. Once Cupcakes are completely cool, use a sharp knife to cut a hole, 1" in diameter and 1" deep, out of the middle of each. Reserve the removed cake pieces.

3. Scoop 1 tablespoon fudge sauce into each hole. Invert removed cake pieces and place on top of the fudge sauce in each Cupcake.

For Buttercream Frosting

½ cup salted butter, softened
3 cups confectioners' sugar
1 tablespoon heavy cream
1 teaspoon vanilla extract

1. In the bowl of a stand mixer, add butter, confectioners' sugar, cream, and vanilla. Using the flat beater attachment, cream together well. Scoop into a large piping bag with a round tip.

2. Starting around the top of one cupcake wrapper, pipe Buttercream Frosting in a circle around the Cupcake and continue swirling up until you reach the point of the cake. Repeat with each Cupcake. Chill 30 minutes.

For Topping

2 cups milk chocolate chips
20 Butterfinger Minis candy bars, finely crushed

1. In a medium microwave-safe bowl, add chocolate chips. Microwave on high 30 seconds, stir, then microwave 15 seconds. Repeat microwaving in 15-second increments, stirring between each, until chocolate has just melted.

2. Spoon chocolate over Buttercream Frosting on each Cupcake and smooth over the surface so that all frosting is covered While the chocolate is still wet, sprinkle and press crushed Butterfinger Minis pieces all over chocolate. Let the chocolate sit for about 30 minutes until it hardens. Store in an airtight container at room temperature up to 3 days.

COOKING TIP

Sometimes grocery stores have "bulk bins" where you can buy ingredients in whatever quantity you like, often for a huge discount off packaged varieties. Take a look at these bins next time you are at the store and see if they have crushed up Butterfingers. It's a great way for the candy bar company to make a little money off bits they would have thrown away— and a sweet deal for you!

Pretzels with Cream Cheese Filling

An Incredible Celebration, Disney's Hollywood Studios

· · · · ✳ · · · ·

An Incredible Celebration used to house the entrance of Toy Story Mania!, but at the opening of Toy Story Land, the entrance was changed to the other side of the building to better incorporate the ride to the new land. This area is now best used to take a break from crowds and eat a Pretzel with Cream Cheese Filling. These unassuming snacks are harder to find at Disney than their Mickey-faced counterparts, but now you can enjoy them whenever you want right at home!

SERVES 4

2 cups warm water (110°F)
1 (¼-ounce) packet active dry yeast
5 cups all-purpose flour
1 tablespoon salt
4 cups room-temperature water
8 ounces cream cheese, softened
1 cup confectioners' sugar
¼ cup baking soda
1 large egg, beaten
1 graham cracker, finely crushed

1. In the bowl of a stand mixer, pour 2 cups warm water and sprinkle yeast on top. Let sit 10 minutes.

2. Add flour and salt to yeast mixture. Using the dough hook attachment, knead 5 minutes. Dough should be smooth and elastic.

3. Remove dough and spray bowl with nonstick cooking spray. Return dough to bowl. Cover with plastic wrap and let rise in a warm place 45 minutes.

4. Preheat oven to 450°F. Line a large ungreased baking sheet with parchment paper and set aside.

5. In a large pot over high heat, bring room-temperature water to a boil.

6. In the bowl of a stand mixer, add cream cheese and confectioners' sugar. Using the flat beater attachment, beat on medium until well combined. Scoop into a large piping bag. Cut a small hole in the tip of the bag. Set aside.

7. Turn dough out onto a clean surface. Cut into four equal pieces. Working with one piece at a time, roll dough into a rope about 25" long. Use a rolling pin to flatten the rope to about 2" width. Pipe cream cheese mixture down the center of the dough, about the thickness of a pencil. Use your fingers to pinch the dough around the cream cheese, making sure dough is sealed tight to avoid spillage.

8. Hold one dough rope up in a *U* shape. Cross the top pieces over one another and twist. Bring them back down toward you and press into the bottom of the *U*. Repeat with remaining dough.

9. Add baking soda to pot of boiling water. Working with one pretzel at a time, use a slotted spoon to slide pretzel into baking soda bath and poach 30 seconds. Remove to prepared baking sheet. Repeat with remaining pretzels.

10. Brush each pretzel with beaten egg and sprinkle on crushed graham cracker crumbs. Bake until pretzels are golden brown, about 12 minutes.

DID YOU KNOW?

The famous company Philadelphia Cream Cheese is not from Philadelphia. The inventor made his cheese in upstate New York, but named it as such because the Philadelphia area had a great reputation as being a dairy heartland.

Mickey Pretzels

An Incredible Celebration, Disney's Hollywood Studios

· · · · ✦ · · ·

These pretzels are sold at Disney's Hollywood Studios in the iconic shape of Mickey's face, but you can get creative with other Disney-inspired shapes in your own kitchen. Cutting the dough, rather than twisting it like traditional pretzels, allows for more creativity and fun. Kids can use cookie cutters or plastic knives to score their shapes, while an adult makes the final sharp cuts. Also, feel free to get wild with the toppings! Try cinnamon sugar or Everything Bagel seasoning.

SERVES 4

1½ cups warm water (110°F)
1 (¼-ounce) packet active dry yeast
2 tablespoons light brown sugar
1 teaspoon salt
4 cups all-purpose flour
4 cups plus 1 tablespoon room-temperature water, divided
¼ cup baking soda
1 large egg
4 teaspoons kosher salt

1. In the bowl of a stand mixer, add warm water and sprinkle yeast on top. Let sit 10 minutes.

2. Add brown sugar and 1 teaspoon salt. Using the flat beater attachment, beat on low speed to combine. Mix in flour. Switch to dough hook attachment and knead 5 minutes. Dough should be smooth and elastic.

3. Remove dough and spray bowl with nonstick cooking spray. Return dough to bowl. Cover with a cloth and let rise in a warm place 30 minutes.

4. Preheat oven to 450°F. Line a large ungreased baking sheet with parchment paper and set aside.

5. In a large pot over high heat, bring 4 cups water to a boil.

6. Turn dough out onto a lightly floured surface. Cut dough into eight equal pieces. Working with one piece at a time, roll dough into a rough heart shape. Using a sharp knife, lightly score or scrape the Mickey shape into the dough. Once you've achieved your desired shape, cut all the way through the dough.

(continued) ▶

7. Add baking soda to pot of boiling water. Working with 1 Mickey at a time, use a big flat spatula to carefully lift a dough Mickey into baking soda bath, and poach 15 seconds. Remove to prepared baking sheet.

8. In a small bowl, mix together egg and remaining 1 tablespoon water. Brush onto Mickeys. Sprinkle kosher salt over pretzels.

9. Bake until deep golden brown, about 10 minutes. Serve immediately.

DID YOU KNOW?

The Mickey Pretzel is most famously sold on Main Street, U.S.A., in Magic Kingdom, but you can actually find this snack at every Disney Park in California and Florida. Carbs for the win!

Chocolate-Hazelnut Lunch Box Tarts

Toy Story Land, Disney's Hollywood Studios

· · · ✦ · · ·

Toy Story Land is a unique experience. Each guest is "shrunk down to the size of a toy" in Andy's backyard. Giant footprints mark the ground, fences are made with used Popsicle sticks (you can even see what color the Popsicles were before they were eaten!), and toys are everywhere. And what is more reminiscent of childhood than eating a Lunch Box Tart? You may even be inspired to revisit some of your favorite toys.

SERVES 6

1 (17.3-ounce) box frozen puff pastry sheets
¾ cup chocolate-hazelnut spread
1 large egg
1 tablespoon room-temperature water
1 cup confectioners' sugar
2 tablespoons heavy cream
2 tablespoons cooked bacon bits

1. Allow pastry to thaw at room temperature 40 minutes. Preheat oven to 400°F. Line a large ungreased baking sheet with parchment paper and set aside.

2. Cut 1 sheet puff pastry into six rectangular pieces. Place 2 tablespoons chocolate hazelnut spread in the middle of each piece, keeping the edges clean.

3. In a small bowl, beat egg and water together with a fork and brush along the clean edges of each pastry piece. Reserve remaining egg wash.

4. Cut second puff pastry sheet into six rectangular pieces. Use your fingers to gently push the middle of the pastry up slightly to accommodate the chocolate-hazelnut spread. Place 1 plain pastry rectangle on top of each chocolate-hazelnut pastry and gently press the edges of each tart together with your fingers. Finish by crimping the edges with a fork.

5. Brush remaining egg wash over each tart. Lay the tarts on prepared baking sheet. Bake until golden brown, about 18 minutes. Allow tarts to cool completely after baking, about 1 hour.

6. In a small bowl, whisk together confectioners' sugar and cream. Spread 1 tablespoon onto each tart. Top with crumbled bacon. Eat immediately.

Lemon-Blueberry Lunch Box Tarts

Toy Story Land, Disney's Hollywood Studios

· · · · ✦ · · ·

Toy Story Land is all about the details: The price tag on Rex's box reads $19.95—like 1995, the year the original *Toy Story* movie came out in theaters. Also, Wheezy's box doesn't say "Wheezy" on it, since that is the name Andy gave to his own "Squeaking Penguin Toy." These Lemon-Blueberry Lunch Box Tarts were created as the perfect snack to carry-and-go while appreciating all the little details around Toy Story Land. Now they can also be made at home as a special treat in family members' lunch boxes!

SERVES 6

1 (17.3-ounce) box frozen puff pastry sheets
¾ cup canned lemon pie filling
1 cup fresh blueberries
1 large egg
1 tablespoon room-temperature water
1 cup confectioners' sugar
1 tablespoon heavy cream
1 tablespoon lemon juice

1. Allow pastry to thaw at room temperature 40 minutes. Preheat oven to 400°F. Line an ungreased baking sheet with parchment paper and set aside.

2. Cut 1 sheet puff pastry into six rectangular pieces. Place 2 tablespoons pie filling on the middle of each piece, keeping the edges clean. Place 6 fresh blueberries into the lemon cream on each pastry piece.

3. In a small bowl, beat egg and water together with a fork. Brush along the clean edges of pastry pieces. Reserve remaining egg wash.

4. Cut second puff pastry sheet into six rectangular pieces. Use your fingers to gently push the middle of the pastry up slightly to accommodate the lemon and blueberries. Place one plain pastry piece on top of each lemon and blueberry pastry and gently press the edges of each tart together with your fingers. Finish by crimping the edges with a fork.

5. Brush remaining egg wash over each tart. Lay tarts on prepared baking sheet. Bake until golden brown, about 18 minutes. Allow tarts to completely cool after baking, about 1 hour.

6. In a small bowl, whisk together confectioners' sugar, cream, and lemon juice. Spread 1 tablespoon onto each tart. Eat immediately.

Green Milk

Star Wars: Galaxy's Edge, Disney's Hollywood Studios

. . . ✦ . . .

Green Milk is first seen in the Star Wars movies in *The Last Jedi,* when Luke Skywalker literally milks the green stuff straight from the space cow! Here is a fun tip: Try mixing your Blue and Green Milks together. Green Milk has a very distinct flavor from the Blue, with more flowery overtones. Locals say the fruity and flowery combination is tastier than one or the other alone!

SERVES 2

1 cup pulp-free orange juice
1 cup passion fruit juice
½ cup canned coconut milk
½ cup rice milk
¼ cup light corn syrup
3 drops lime green gel food coloring

In a blender, add all ingredients and blend until well combined. Pour into an ice cream machine. Follow manufacturer's instructions and run about 8 minutes or until slushy. Enjoy immediately.

Blue Milk

Star Wars: Galaxy's Edge, Disney's Hollywood Studios

· · · · ✦ · · ·

It was a unique challenge for the designers of Galaxy's Edge to create a flavor to match the iconic look of Blue Milk from the Star Wars movies. Instead of coming up with something predictable—like a milk flavor—they swung the other direction and dreamed up a flavor no one would expect! This fruity, slushy drink has been a go-to at the park ever since.

SERVES 2

1 cup pineapple juice
½ cup rice milk
½ cup canned coconut milk
½ cup passion fruit juice
1 tablespoon lime juice
1 tablespoon watermelon syrup
2 drops blue gel food coloring

In a blender, add all ingredients and blend until well combined. Pour into an ice cream machine. Follow manufacturer's instructions and run about 8 minutes or until slushy. Enjoy immediately.

DID YOU KNOW?

Mark Hamill (the actor who played Luke Skywalker) said the Blue Milk they used on set for Star Wars: A New Hope *was shelf-stable milk and triggered his gag reflex. This version is far more palatable!*

Outpost Popcorn Mix

Star Wars: Galaxy's Edge, Disney's Hollywood Studios

· · · · ✦ · · ·

At Kat Saka's Kettle, you can grab a Mouse Droid full of Outpost Popcorn Mix. Unlike most popcorns available at Disney Parks, this dish has two flavors mixed together to create one amazing snack. Fans have described this crazy flavor combo as similar to Fruity Pebbles cereal. Even better, the Mouse Droid container it comes in is not only a handy case for your popcorn, but also makes a great souvenir to take home after your vacation. When you make this mix at home, fill that Mouse Droid up again and again!

SERVES 6

For Spicy Popcorn

½ cup cold salted butter
2 (5-ounce) boxes Hot Tamales candy
½ cup granulated sugar
½ cup light corn syrup
1 teaspoon salt
½ teaspoon baking soda
12 cups popped plain popcorn

1. Preheat oven to 225°F. Line four ungreased baking sheets with parchment paper and set aside.

2. In a medium saucepan over medium heat, add butter, Hot Tamales candy, sugar, corn syrup, and salt. Stir well to combine. Continue to stir until temperature reaches 280°F. Remove from heat and stir in baking soda.

3. Pour half popcorn into a large paper grocery bag. Pour half spicy sauce over the popcorn. Add remaining popcorn, then remaining sauce. Fold down top of bag and, while wearing oven mitts, shake vigorously 30 seconds.

4. Pour popcorn onto two of the prepared baking sheets. Bake 45 minutes, stirring every 15 minutes. Remove from oven to cool on baking sheet 30 minutes.

For Sweet Popcorn

½ cup cold salted butter
⅓ cup light corn syrup
1 (3-ounce) box grape-
  flavored gelatin mix
½ cup granulated sugar
½ teaspoon baking soda
16 cups popped plain
  popcorn

1. In a medium microwave-safe bowl, add butter, corn syrup, gelatin mix, and sugar. Do not stir. Microwave on high for 2 minutes. Stir. Microwave an additional 3 minutes. Stir in baking soda.

2. Pour half popcorn into a large paper grocery bag. Pour half sweet sauce onto the popcorn. Add remaining popcorn, then remaining sauce. Fold down the top of the bag and put bag into microwave. Cook 1 minute. Remove bag and shake 30 seconds. Microwave an additional 1 minute. Shake 30 seconds more. Microwave another 20 seconds.

3. Pour popcorn onto remaining prepared baking sheets and allow to cool 30 minutes.

4. Once both popcorn batches have cooled, mix together in a large bowl. Store in an airtight container at room temperature up to 3 days.

Ronto Wraps

Star Wars: Galaxy's Edge, Disney's Hollywood Studios

· · · · ✦ · · ·

When you step up to Ronto Roasters in Galaxy's Edge, you'll be met with a gigantic podracer engine that is cooking the meats. Well, not really, but it sure does look like it! While these Ronto Wraps are made like the original recipe, you can also re-create the breakfast and vegan versions sold at Star Wars: Galaxy's Edge. For a Ronto Morning Wrap, fill your pita with scrambled eggs, pork sausage, and cheese. And to make the Ronto-less Wrap, whip up some vegan sausage and top with kimchi and cucumbers.

SERVES 6

For Peppercorn Sauce

- 1 medium English cucumber, peeled and grated
- 1 teaspoon salt
- 2 cups low-fat plain Greek-style yogurt
- Juice of ½ large lemon
- 4 medium cloves garlic, peeled and minced
- 1 teaspoon dried dill weed
- 1 teaspoon chopped fresh mint
- 2 teaspoons cracked black peppercorns

1. In a medium bowl, add cucumber and sprinkle with salt. Let sit 10 minutes, then place in a cloth or paper towel and squeeze out all the liquid.

2. In a separate large bowl, add yogurt, lemon juice, garlic, dill, mint, and peppercorns. Whisk to combine. Add cucumber and mix thoroughly. Cover and refrigerate until ready to use.

COOKING TIP

This recipe can be a bit labor-intensive, but if you're looking for a quick lunch, here are some shortcuts to make these wraps in a snap: Use a preshredded coleslaw mix and bottled tzatziki sauce for the Slaw and Peppercorn Sauce; get precooked sausages so they heat up quickly; skip the pork.

(continued) ▸

For Slaw

1 cup thin strips red cabbage
½ cup sliced carrots
1 cup thin strips green cabbage
½ cup sliced red onion
3 tablespoons apple cider vinegar
1 teaspoon Dijon mustard
1 tablespoon olive oil
1 teaspoon dried basil
2 teaspoons granulated sugar
¼ teaspoon salt
¼ teaspoon ground black pepper

In a medium bowl, mix together red cabbage, carrots, green cabbage, and onion. In a separate small bowl, mix together remaining ingredients. Pour over vegetables and stir. Cover and refrigerate until ready to use.

For Wraps

6 (2.5-ounce) thin-cut pork chops
¼ teaspoon salt
¼ teaspoon ground black pepper
6 (6"-long) pork sausages
6 pita breads

1. Preheat grill or grill pan to medium heat. Season pork chops with salt and pepper and grill 4 minutes on each side.

2. Remove chops to a cutting board. Cook sausages on grill over medium heat until cooked through and hot, about 8 minutes.

3. Remove sausages to cutting board. Grill pita bread over medium heat until toasty, about 2 minutes.

4. Place 1 pork chop, 1 sausage, and one-sixth Slaw on pita bread and top with one-sixth Peppercorn Sauce. Fold into a taco. Repeat with remaining ingredients and serve immediately.

Peanut Butter and Jelly Milk Shakes

Echo Lake, Disney's Hollywood Studios

· · · · ✦ · · ·

The 50's Prime Time Café, where this rich, nostalgic-tasting shake is served, is a table service restaurant well known for the "harassment" the servers dish out to the guests. Each server puts on a persona as a strict aunt or uncle who is having you over to their house. Don't forget to wash your hands before dinner, put your napkin on your lap, and keep your elbows off the table. But not to worry: You don't have to eat all your greens before enjoying a Peanut Butter and Jelly Milk Shake at home!

SERVES 2

3 cups vanilla ice cream
¼ cup whole milk
¼ cup creamy peanut butter
3 tablespoons grape jelly

In a blender, add all ingredients and blend until smooth.

MIX IT UP

Don't have any grape jelly? Use any kind you want! This shake tastes great with strawberry, raspberry, apricot—just about any jelly. Try new flavors and see what you like best.

Frozen Chocolate-Covered Bananas

Echo Lake, Disney's Hollywood Studios

· · · · ✦ · · ·

The best way to enjoy a frozen banana at Disney is at Echo Lake. You can catch the Indiana Jones Epic Stunt Spectacular! several times a day here; pick up your frozen banana and take it to the show! And when you make this recipe at home, you can customize it however you want. Not a fan of nuts? Try shredded coconut, crushed M&M's, white chocolate, caramel, or sprinkles.

SERVES 6

3 large just-underripe bananas, peeled and cut in half
1 cup milk chocolate chips
1 cup dark chocolate chips
1 cup semisweet chocolate chips
1 tablespoon coconut oil
1 cup chopped salted dry-roasted peanuts

1. Line an ungreased baking sheet with parchment paper. Carefully push a Popsicle stick into the flat, cut end of each banana. Place bananas on prepared baking sheet and freeze 1 hour.

2. In a large microwave-safe bowl, add all chocolate chips and coconut oil. Microwave on high 30 seconds, stir, then microwave 15 seconds. Repeat microwaving in 15-second increments, stirring between each, until chocolate is melted and smooth.

3. Remove baking sheet from freezer and dip one banana into chocolate to fully coat. Quickly sprinkle with peanuts and return to baking sheet. Repeat with remaining bananas.

4. Return to freezer for at least 30 minutes before serving.

CHAPTER 7

Disney's Animal Kingdom

Disney's Animal Kingdom used to be considered a "half-day" park when it first opened, but now it is anything but! This amusement-park-meets-zoo is thrilling from sunup to sundown. Begin your day with famous Mickey Waffles at Tusker House in Africa before you head out on Kilimanjaro Safaris. A midday cooldown on Kali River Rapids in Asia (and a heat-up with Mr. Kamal's Seasoned Fries) is essential. And of course, don't miss a stop at Pandora—The World of Avatar. Pick up a Night Blossom drink to sip at some point too. Is your stomach growling yet? Fear not! In this chapter, you'll find every recipe you need to re-create the wild magic of Disney's Animal Kingdom at home. Whip up Baked Lobster Macaroni & Cheese to wow guests, or enjoy a tasty batch of Blueberry Cream Cheese Mousse with your family while watching (or rewatching) the *Avatar* movie.

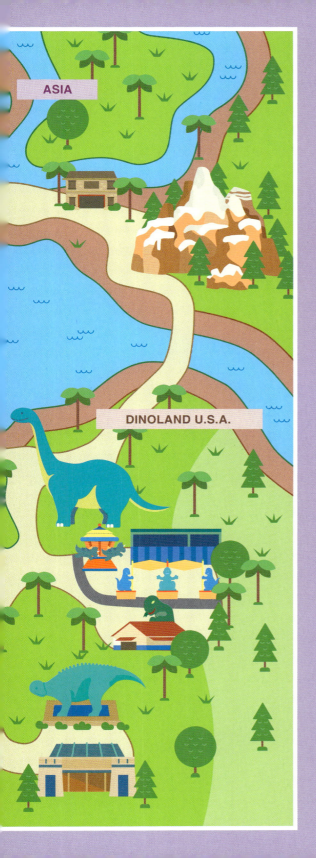

★ 1 **MICKEY WAFFLES** *(Africa, Disney's Animal Kingdom)*

★ 2 **HAYSTACKS** *(Africa, Disney's Animal Kingdom)*

★ 3 **NIGHT BLOSSOMS** *(Pandora—The World of Avatar, Disney's Animal Kingdom)*

★ 4 **CHEESEBURGER STEAMED PODS** *(Pandora—The World of Avatar, Disney's Animal Kingdom)*

★ 5 **BLUEBERRY CREAM CHEESE MOUSSE** *(Pandora—The World of Avatar, Disney's Animal Kingdom)*

★ 6 **PONGU LUMPIA** *(Pandora—The World of Avatar, Disney's Animal Kingdom)*

★ 7 **MR. KAMAL'S SEASONED FRIES** *(Asia, Disney's Animal Kingdom)*

★ 8 **FROZEN LEMONADE** *(Discovery Island, Disney's Animal Kingdom)*

★ 9 **MICKEY ICE CREAM SANDWICHES** *(Discovery Island, Disney's Animal Kingdom)*

★ 10 **MICKEY ICE CREAM BARS** *(Discovery Island, Disney's Animal Kingdom)*

★ 11 **FRENCH FRIES WITH PULLED PORK AND CHEESE** *(Discovery Island, Disney's Animal Kingdom)*

★ 12 **BAKED MACARONI & CHEESE WITH PULLED PORK** *(Discovery Island, Disney's Animal Kingdom)*

★ 13 **BAKED LOBSTER MACARONI & CHEESE** *(Discovery Island, Disney's Animal Kingdom)*

Mickey Waffles

Africa, Disney's Animal Kingdom

· · · · ✦ · · ·

Mickey Waffles are a classic part of the Disney experience—not just because of the delicious taste, but also because of the iconic Mickey Mouse shape. In Disney's Animal Kingdom, Africa, they are sometimes served at Tusker House Restaurant in the shapes of Simba and Nala! Whether you are heading out on safari or creating your own adventures at home, they are the perfect meal to fuel your day. For the authentic Mickey shape, you can order a Mickey waffle iron from ShopDisney.com.

SERVES 10

2 large eggs, separated
½ cup vegetable oil
2 cups whole milk
1 teaspoon vanilla extract
2 cups all-purpose flour
4 teaspoons baking powder
¼ teaspoon salt
¼ cup granulated sugar
¼ cup salted butter, melted

1. Preheat waffle iron.

2. In the bowl of a stand mixer, add egg whites. Using the whisk attachment, whip on high until stiff peaks form, about 5 minutes.

3. In a separate large bowl, whisk together egg yolks, oil, milk, and vanilla. Add flour, baking powder, salt, and sugar, and mix until combined. Using a spatula, gently fold in egg whites.

4. Preheat oven to 175°F and place a wire cooling rack on a baking sheet. Place baking sheet in oven.

5. Use a brush to lightly spread a little melted butter onto waffle iron. Scoop ¼ cup batter into waffle iron and cook according to the manufacturer's instructions.

6. When waffle is done, remove from waffle iron and place on wire rack on baking sheet in oven. Repeat with remaining batter.

DID YOU KNOW?

Mickey Waffles are so popular worldwide that whole merchandise lines revolve around them, including dog chew toys, magnets, air fresheners, coin purses, key chains, candles, and T-shirts.

Haystacks

Africa, Disney's Animal Kingdom

· · · ✦ · · ·

This unique treat is sold only in Africa at Disney's Animal Kingdom. While not actually African, it is inspired by the Zangbeto, voodoo deities who are "night watchmen" for groups in Benin, Togo, and Nigeria. The Zangbeto dress in elaborate costumes that look like giant haystacks.

SERVES 6

3 cups mini-marshmallows
½ cup creamy peanut butter
3 tablespoons cold salted butter
3 cups shoestring potato sticks

1. Line an ungreased baking sheet with parchment paper. Grease with nonstick cooking spray and set aside.

2. In a large microwave-safe bowl, combine marshmallows, peanut butter, and butter. Microwave on high 30 seconds. Stir. Microwave 30 seconds more. Stir. Pour in potato sticks and stir until well combined.

3. Scoop ½-cup portions onto prepared baking sheet. Cover.

4. Place tray in refrigerator and chill 30 minutes before serving.

COOKING TIP

If you don't have a microwave, or prefer not to use it for this recipe, it can be made on the stovetop. Just combine marshmallows, peanut butter, and butter in a large saucepan over medium heat until all ingredients are totally melted, then stir in potato sticks and chill as instructed.

Night Blossoms

Pandora—The World of Avatar, Disney's Animal Kingdom

· · · ✦ · · ·

The Night Blossom is a delicious non-alcoholic beverage with a lot to love. Frozen layers of flavor are refreshing on a hot day, while the boba balls lend a fun texture and little pops of fun in every sip. If you want to learn more about the crazy plants and animals you see and hear around Pandora, just find an Alpha Centauri Expeditions (ACE) Field Guide. They give lots of information about the alien planet, such as how many of the plants have an animal-like nervous system, which plants explode seeds if touched, or where to view bioluminescence at night.

SERVES 2

2 cups limeade
½ cup apple juice concentrate
1 cup strawberry watermelon juice
2 drops pink gel food coloring
1 drop purple gel food coloring
1 cup lime sherbet
¼ cup lemon-lime soda
½ cup passion fruit boba balls

1. Mix together limeade, apple juice concentrate, and strawberry watermelon juice. Pour into an ice cream machine and run 8 minutes, or until slushy. Mix in pink and purple food coloring.

2. Meanwhile, use a blender to blend together lime sherbet and lemon-lime soda.

3. Divide ½ pink limeade mix into the bottom of two large glasses. Add ½ green mix to each, then layer on remaining pink mix. Top with passion fruit boba balls.

COOKING TIP

Boba balls are difficult to make, but easy to purchase. Just go to a local Asian market or bubble tea shop and ask for them. They are sometimes available in fruit cups at the regular grocery store as well. If you can't find them, that's fine too: This drink is delicious with or without boba balls.

Cheeseburger Steamed Pods

Pandora—The World of Avatar, Disney's Animal Kingdom

· · · · ✦ · · ·

Arguably the most stunning feature of the Pandora landscape is the floating mountains held aloft in the Valley of Mo'ara. These 156-foot wonders look to be actually floating in the air but are in fact held up by steel beams. And with stunning attractions comes equally stunning—and mouthwatering—meals. These Cheeseburger Steamed Pods look positively out of this world! Whip up a batch for family dinner or serve at your next party to wow guests.

SERVES 6

For Pod Buns

2 cups all-purpose flour
½ teaspoon active dry yeast
1 cup warm water (110°F)

1. In the bowl of a stand mixer, add flour and yeast. Using dough hook attachment, beat on medium to mix. Slowly pour in warm water while mixing. Knead dough 5 minutes.

2. Grease a large bowl with nonstick cooking spray. Transfer dough to greased bowl. Cover with plastic wrap and let rise in a warm place until doubled in size, about 1 hour.

For Cheeseburger Filling

1 tablespoon vegetable oil
½ medium yellow onion, peeled and diced
1 teaspoon minced garlic
1 pound ground beef
1 teaspoon salt
1 teaspoon ground black pepper
1 tablespoon yellow mustard
1 tablespoon ketchup
2 cups shredded Cheddar cheese

1. In a large skillet over medium heat, heat oil 30 seconds, then add onion and garlic. Cook 2 minutes. Add ground beef, salt, and pepper. Cook until beef is no longer pink, about 6 minutes. Remove from heat and drain.

2. Stir mustard and ketchup into beef and set aside.

3. Line a steamer basket with a circle of parchment paper. Fill a large pot with 2" water and place prepared steamer basket on top. Over high heat, bring water to a boil.

4. Turn risen dough out onto a floured surface. Gently roll into a log about 12" long. Cut off a golf ball–sized piece of dough and flatten with a rolling pin. Hold the dough in your palm and scoop in 2 tablespoons meat filling into center. Sprinkle 1 tablespoon cheese on top of the meat. Use your opposite hand to carefully fold and crimp the top of the bun shut. Place in steamer basket. Repeat with remaining dough and fillings until basket is full, then place a lid on top and steam 15 minutes. Turn the heat off and let rest in the covered steamer 5 minutes more.

5. Remove pods to a serving tray and place in oven to maintain warmth. Repeat cooking with any remaining dough and fillings.

Blueberry Cream Cheese Mousse

Pandora—The World of Avatar, Disney's Animal Kingdom

· · · · ✦ · · ·

These Blueberry Cream Cheese Mousse desserts transport you to *Avatar*'s beautiful alien planet, Pandora, any day of the week. The unique blend of textures makes it hard to place each ingredient. Your friends will certainly be impressed when you show up to the next gathering with these!

SERVES 6

For Blueberry Mousse

1 cup fresh or frozen blueberries
½ cup granulated sugar
1 teaspoon salt
1 cup sour cream
8 ounces cream cheese, softened
1 cup heavy cream
6 (3½") soft sugar cookies

1. Grease a jumbo muffin pan with nonstick cooking spray. Line with disks of plastic wrap and set aside.

2. In a large saucepan over medium heat, add blueberries, sugar, and salt. Cook 10 minutes.

3. In a food processor, add blueberry mixture and allow to cool 15 minutes. Add sour cream and cream cheese. Pulse until well mixed. Set aside.

4. In the bowl of a stand mixer, add heavy cream. Using the whisk attachment, beat on high until stiff peaks form. Fold blueberry mixture into whipped cream.

5. Fill each jumbo muffin cup with Blueberry Mousse. Tap pan onto countertop to shake mousse down into the cups. Top each filled cup with 1 sugar cookie. Freeze until solid, at least 6 hours or overnight.

(continued) ▶

For Passion Fruit Curd

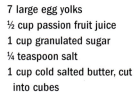

7 large egg yolks
½ cup passion fruit juice
1 cup granulated sugar
¼ teaspoon salt
1 cup cold salted butter, cut into cubes

1. In a medium saucepan over medium heat, add egg yolks, passion fruit juice, sugar, and salt. When bubbles begin to form, reduce heat to a simmer. Whisk continuously until mixture thickens, about 8 minutes.

2. Remove from heat and stir in butter, 1 cube at a time, until butter is melted and fully incorporated. Pour curd through a sieve into a medium bowl. Refrigerate covered until completely firm, at least 6 hours or overnight.

For Glaze

2 tablespoons plus ½ cup room-temperature water, divided
1 tablespoon unflavored gelatin
¾ cup granulated sugar
⅓ cup sweetened condensed milk
1 cup white chocolate chips
2 drops bright blue gel food coloring

1. In a small bowl, mix 2 tablespoons water with gelatin. Set aside.

2. In a medium microwave-safe bowl, add sugar, remaining ½ cup water, and sweetened condensed milk. Microwave on high 1 minute and stir. Add gelatin mix and whisk well to combine.

3. In a separate medium microwave-safe bowl, add chocolate chips. Microwave on high 30 seconds, stir, then microwave 15 seconds. Repeat microwaving in 15-second increments, stirring between each, until chocolate melts. Pour chocolate into gelatin mixture and whisk until well combined. Add food coloring. Allow to cool to 90°F.

For Topping

Canned whipped cream

Place a wire cooling rack on a baking sheet. Remove Blueberry Mousse from muffin tin and place inverted (cookie-side down) on wire rack. Pour Glaze over each mousse. Once the Glaze stops dripping, transfer mousse to serving plates. Scoop ¼ cup Passion Fruit Curd on top of each serving. Top with a swirl of whipped cream.

DID YOU KNOW?

Imagineer Joe Rohde, who created the land of Pandora—The World of Avatar for the park, said that every land at Disney is about storytelling, no matter the subject matter. So whether it be a trip to colonial America, living the golden age of Hollywood, or stepping into the alien environment of Pandora, enjoy your experience and allow yourself to be transported!

Pongu Lumpia

Pandora—The World of Avatar, Disney's Animal Kingdom

· · · ✦ · · ·

Although these lumpia are served on the otherworldly planet of Pandora, they actually originate from the Philippines on planet Earth. They come in sweet, savory, fried, and fresh varieties. You can roll almost anything up into these yummy wraps. Pair these sweet treats with a Night Blossom (see recipe in this chapter) and you'll feel like a member of the Alpha Centauri Expeditions team in no time!

YIELDS 10 ROLLS

3 cups vegetable oil for frying
1 large egg
1 teaspoon room-temperature water
10 egg roll wrappers
8 ounces cream cheese, softened
1 (20-ounce) can pineapple chunks packed in juice, drained
½ cup granulated sugar, divided

1. In a medium, heavy-bottomed pot over medium-high heat, add vegetable oil. It should measure to a depth of about 2". Heat until oil reaches 350°F. Line a large plate with paper towels and set aside.

2. In a small bowl, beat egg and water together with a fork. Lay 1 egg roll wrapper in front of you. Brush egg wash onto two adjacent sides of egg roll wrapper. Spread a thin layer of cream cheese across the non-egg-washed surface of the wrapper. Place 4 chunks pineapple in a line in the center of the wrapper. Sprinkle 1 teaspoon sugar onto the pineapple. Roll up like a burrito, making sure the egg-washed edges are the last thing to roll up. Repeat with remaining wrappers to make ten rolls.

3. Carefully slide three rolls into the hot oil. Fry until golden brown, about 4 minutes, turning frequently. Remove to lined plate. Repeat with remaining rolls.

4. Sprinkle remaining sugar over the outside of the hot rolls.

Mr. Kamal's Seasoned Fries

Asia, Disney's Animal Kingdom

· · · · ✦ · · · ·

Mr. Kamal's Seasoned Fries are a yummy midday snack at Animal Kingdom to chase away the hunger of the afternoon. The high-carb content will give kids and adults some energy to explore their way through Asia—or have fun a little closer to home.

SERVES 5

- 4 cups vegetable oil for frying
- 5 large russet potatoes, peeled and cut into fries
- ¼ teaspoon paprika
- ¼ cup salt
- 3 tablespoons garlic powder
- 1 teaspoon chili powder
- 1 teaspoon onion powder
- ½ teaspoon ground black pepper
- ½ teaspoon ground cumin
- ¼ teaspoon celery salt
- ½ cup ketchup
- 2 tablespoons sriracha sauce
- 3 tablespoons amber honey
- ¼ cup tzatziki sauce

1. Preheat oven to 200°F. Line an ungreased baking sheet with parchment paper and set aside.

2. In a medium pot over medium-high heat, add vegetable oil to reach a depth of about 3". Heat until oil reaches 375°F. Line a large plate with paper towels.

3. Working in batches, carefully slide fries into the hot oil. Cook until light brown, about 5 minutes. Remove to lined plate and allow to drain 3 minutes.

4. Transfer fries to prepared baking sheet and place in oven to keep warm while cooking remaining fries.

5. In a large bowl, add paprika, salt, garlic powder, chili powder, onion powder, pepper, cumin, and celery salt. Stir to mix. Toss fries with seasoning.

6. In a separate small bowl, stir together ketchup, sriracha, and honey.

7. Top fries with tzatziki sauce and drizzle with sriracha ketchup.

MIX IT UP

Sriracha ketchup can be a bit on the fiery hot side, so if that's not to your taste, feel free to sub it for something that you do love. Exchange the sriracha for barbecue sauce and combine with the ketchup and honey to create a markedly sweeter snack.

Frozen Lemonade

Discovery Island, Disney's Animal Kingdom

· · · ✦ · · ·

Disney Parks have served three different varieties of Frozen Lemonade over the years: original lemon, strawberry, and orangeade. If you want to try the other two varieties at home, follow the freezing directions below, but add premade strawberry lemonade or orange juice to your ice cream machine instead of the lemonade.

SERVES 4

1¾ cups granulated sugar
8 cups room-temperature water, divided
1½ cups lemon juice
5 drops yellow gel food coloring

1. In a medium microwave-safe bowl, combine sugar and 1 cup water. Microwave 1 minute, stir, then microwave 1 more minute and stir to create a syrup. Cover and refrigerate until cool, about 2 hours.

2. In a large bowl or pitcher, stir together syrup, lemon juice, remaining 7 cups water, and yellow food coloring.

3. Pour lemonade into an ice cream machine. Follow manufacturer's instructions and run 15 minutes or until slushy.

4. Pour lemonade into medium-tall plastic cups. Freeze 5 hours until frozen solid.

COOKING TIP

The Frozen Lemonade at Disney is Minute Maid brand. So if you want the exact authentic flavor, buy a bottle of Minute Maid lemonade from your local grocery store and follow these freezing instructions.

Mickey Ice Cream Sandwiches

Discovery Island, Disney's Animal Kingdom

• • • ✦ • • •

Discovery Island is home to the Tree of Life, the central hub of Animal Kingdom. Made out of an oil rig skeleton, it is designed to withstand hurricane-force winds (which are not terribly uncommon in Florida). The perfect pick-me-up after a hurricane (or just a long day of work), these sandwiches have soft chocolate cookies on either side of a creamy vanilla ice cream. They're a sweet tooth's dream!

SERVES 6

⅓ cup salted butter,
 softened
1 tablespoon shortening
1 cup granulated sugar
2 large eggs
1 teaspoon vanilla extract
1½ cups all-purpose flour
½ cup cocoa powder
½ teaspoon salt
¼ teaspoon baking powder
½ gallon vanilla ice cream

1. Preheat oven to 350°F. Line a large ungreased baking sheet with parchment paper and set aside.

2. In the bowl of a stand mixer, add butter, shortening, sugar, eggs, and vanilla. Using the flat beater attachment, cream together well. Add flour, cocoa powder, salt, and baking powder. Mix until well combined.

3. Using two sizes of cookie scoops, make Mickeys by placing a larger circle of dough onto prepared baking sheet, then adding two "ears" above it with the smaller scoop (you can also use a Mickey cookie cutter). Grease one side of a spatula and flatten scoops slightly. Use fingers to smooth dough between the "ears" and "head" so they connect. Poke circles a few times with a fork to prevent them puffing up.

4. Bake Mickeys 20 minutes, or until bottoms are starting to firm up, then allow to cool completely on the sheet, about 30 minutes.

5. Allow ice cream to soften slightly, about 5 minutes, on the counter. Scoop ice cream onto 1 cookie and top with another cookie. Repeat with remaining cookies and ice cream. Freeze ice cream sandwiches until firm, about 2 hours, or serve immediately.

Mickey Ice Cream Bars

Discovery Island, Disney's Animal Kingdom

· · · ✦ · · ·

These ice cream bars are yummy *and* cooling! The smooth chocolate and mild vanilla ice cream are the classic flavor combination. And who doesn't love a treat on a stick for easy eating? Whip up a batch of these for your next warm-weather party—your guests are sure to be impressed. While the original treat is found on Discovery Island, you can't walk far in Disney without seeing a version of the Mickey Ice Cream Bar for sale.

SERVES 6

½ gallon vanilla ice cream
2 cups semisweet chocolate chips
1 tablespoon coconut oil

1. Microwave ice cream in tub for 1 minute on high.

2. Line an ungreased baking sheet with parchment paper. Scoop out softened ice cream onto baking sheet and spread to ½" thickness.

3. Place baking sheet in freezer and allow to freeze solid, about 4 hours.

4. Use a Mickey cookie cutter to cut Mickey shapes out of the ice cream. If you don't have a Mickey cookie cutter, you can freehand the shape with a knife, or just use the top of a glass to make a circle. Separate the shapes and insert a Popsicle stick into the bottom of each one. Place sheet back in the freezer for 2 hours.

5. In a medium microwave-safe bowl, add chocolate chips and coconut oil. Microwave on high 30 seconds, stir, then microwave 15 seconds. Repeat microwaving in 15-second increments, stirring between each, until chocolate is completely melted and glossy. Allow to cool at room temperature 10 minutes.

6. Line a large plate with parchment paper and set aside.

7. Carefully hold an ice cream bar by the Popsicle stick over the bowl of chocolate. Spoon chocolate over the bar until ice cream is completely covered. Place on lined plate. Repeat with remaining Mickey Ice Cream Bars, then place plate in freezer 30 minutes before serving.

French Fries
with Pulled Pork and Cheese

Discovery Island, Disney's Animal Kingdom

· · · ✦ · · ·

While Disney Parks are known for their crowds, some spots remain relatively tranquil. The Discovery Island Trail that circles the Tree of Life is one such place. You may even spot some wildlife! This special location is just steps from the seating area at Flame Tree Barbecue, where these loaded fries are sold. The combination of nacho cheese and barbecue sauce will bring you back to this recipe time and again.

SERVES 5

3 cups vegetable oil for frying

5 large russet potatoes, peeled and sliced into fries

1 cup canned nacho cheese sauce

Pulled Pork from Baked Macaroni & Cheese with Pulled Pork (see recipe in this chapter)

¼ cup barbecue sauce

1. Preheat oven to 200°F. Line an ungreased baking sheet with parchment paper and set aside.

2. In a medium, heavy-bottomed pot over medium-high heat, add vegetable oil. It should measure to a depth of about 3". Heat until oil reaches 375°F. Line a large paper plate with paper towels and set aside.

3. Working in batches, carefully slide fries into hot oil. Cook until light brown, about 5 minutes. Remove to lined plate and allow to drain 3 minutes.

4. Transfer fries to prepared baking sheet and place sheet in oven to keep warm while cooking remaining fries.

5. Lay a handful of fries on a large plate. Drizzle nacho cheese over fries and pile on the Pulled Pork. Squeeze on some barbecue sauce. Continue layering until all ingredients are used up.

Baked Macaroni & Cheese with Pulled Pork

Discovery Island, Disney's Animal Kingdom

· · · ✦ · · ·

Cast Members at Animal Kingdom have a unique work environment. Every bathroom in the park has doors that open outward only so that if an animal escapes, guests can shelter there. Animal escapes are actually fairly common (usually birds refusing to return to their keepers). Let's hope any doors to your kitchen open outward too, because the scent of this Baked Macaroni & Cheese with Pulled Pork is sure to make anyone go wild!

SERVES 6

For Pulled Pork

- 2 tablespoons vegetable oil
- 1 tablespoon light brown sugar
- 2 teaspoons paprika
- 2 teaspoons garlic powder
- 2 teaspoons onion powder
- 1 teaspoon salt
- 1 teaspoon ground black pepper
- ½ teaspoon ground cumin
- 3 pounds boneless pork roast, cut into 2" cubes
- 1¼ cups beef broth, divided
- ⅓ cup apple cider vinegar
- 2 cups barbecue sauce, divided

1. Heat vegetable oil in electric pressure cooker on the "sauté" function 2 minutes.

2. In a medium bowl, mix together brown sugar, paprika, garlic powder, onion powder, salt, pepper, and cumin. Toss in pork cubes and coat. Add pork to pressure cooker in a single layer. Allow pork to brown about 5 minutes, then flip and brown 5 more minutes.

3. Remove pork from electric pressure cooker and set aside, then deglaze the pot with ¼ cup beef broth, scraping the cooked bits off the bottom.

4. In a large bowl, mix together vinegar, 1 cup barbecue sauce, and remaining 1 cup beef broth. Add pork back to pressure cooker and pour in broth mix. Cover and set to "pressure cook" or "manual." Set cook time for 40 minutes. Allow pressure cooker to naturally release pressure 10 minutes, then quick-release remaining pressure.

5. Remove pork and place into a large dish. Using two forks, shred pork. Mix in remaining 1 cup barbecue sauce. Set aside.

(continued) ▶

For Macaroni & Cheese

3 tablespoons cold salted butter

2 tablespoons all-purpose flour

2 cups whole milk

2 cups shredded sharp Cheddar cheese

2 cups dry elbow pasta, cooked according to package instructions

1½ teaspoons salt

1 teaspoon ground black pepper

1. In a large saucepan over low heat, melt butter. Add flour and cook 2 minutes, stirring continually. Raise heat to medium and add milk. Bring to a boil while continuing to stir. Once boiling, reduce heat to low and simmer 4 minutes.

2. Add cheese and stir until melted and well combined. Pour in pasta and stir until coated. Season with salt and pepper.

3. Spoon Macaroni & Cheese onto serving plates and top with Pulled Pork.

MIX IT UP

Macaroni & cheese is an amazing vehicle for almost any of your favorite ingredients! Try new creations by topping this cheesy goodness with whatever you have in the refrigerator. Some fun ideas include ground beef, fresh peas, cut-up hot dogs, jackfruit, or bacon.

Baked Lobster Macaroni & Cheese

Discovery Island, Disney's Animal Kingdom

· · · ✦ · · ·

Macaroni & cheese is a favorite American comfort food. And why wouldn't it be? The sticky pasta coated in ooey-gooey cheeses hits the spot every time. This dish includes lobster, but if that isn't your thing, feel free to change it up! Consider trying the following add-ins: shrimp, chicken, red beans, or crabmeat. Eight Spoon Café (where the original Baked Lobster Macaroni & Cheese recipe was sold) often changes its own macaroni & cheese lineup, so stop by and see what they are serving during your next visit.

SERVES 6

3 tablespoons cold salted butter

¼ cup all-purpose flour

2 cups whole milk

4 cups shredded sharp white Cheddar cheese, divided

1 teaspoon salt

1 teaspoon garlic powder

1 teaspoon ground black pepper

1 teaspoon onion powder

8 ounces dry elbow macaroni, cooked according to package instructions

½ cup shredded precooked lobster meat

1. Preheat oven to broil on high. Grease the bottom and sides of a 9" × 13" baking pan or six individual oven-safe ramekins with nonstick cooking spray.

2. In a large saucepan over medium heat, add butter and flour. Cook, whisking together, 2 minutes.

3. In a small microwave-safe bowl, microwave milk on high 2 minutes. Whisk milk into flour mixture, still over medium heat. Cook, stirring, 2 minutes more. Remove from heat.

4. Add 3 cups cheese, salt, garlic powder, pepper, and onion powder to milk mixture. Add cooked macaroni and stir until well combined. Stir in lobster meat.

5. Spoon macaroni & cheese into dish(es) and sprinkle with remaining 1 cup cheese.

6. Broil until cheese on top is brown and bubbling, about 8 minutes.

CHAPTER 8

Disney California Adventure

California is a culinary hub of the United States, and Imagineers wanted to convey that in Disney California Adventure. Prominent cultures in the state offer authentic eats at the park. Head directly to Pacific Wharf, where you can pick up meals food court–style from Asian, Mexican, San Franciscan, and Sonoma eateries. From there, Disney-goers can loop around Pixar Pier and sample classic American snacks and treats, such as Chicken Drumsticks, Chili-Lime Corn on the Cob, and of course a warm chocolate chip cookie. But why miss out on these magical offerings when you're not at the parks. In this chapter, you'll find all of the recipes you need to create your own delectable adventures anytime you choose, in the comfort of your home. Cool off on a sunny day with a Mangonada Smoothie, or turn up the heat on a brisk afternoon with Campfire Chili. It's your Disney experience!

1 **MANGONADA SMOOTHIES** (Hollywood Land, Disney California Adventure)

2 **CARNITAS TACOS** (Hollywood Land, Disney California Adventure)

3 **BERRY SCHMOOZIES** (Hollywood Land, Disney California Adventure)

4 **CHURRO TOFFEE** (Buena Vista Street, Disney California Adventure)

5 **PUMPKIN SPICE CHURROS** (Buena Vista Street, Disney California Adventure)

6 **CAMPFIRE CHILI** (Grizzly Peak, Disney California Adventure)

7 **S'MORES** (Grizzly Peak, Disney California Adventure)

8 **COBBLER SHAKES** (Grizzly Peak, Disney California Adventure)

9 **CORN DOGS** (Paradise Gardens Park, Disney California Adventure)

10 **CHICKEN DRUMSTICKS** (Pixar Pier, Disney California Adventure)

11 **CHILI-LIME CORN ON THE COB** (Pixar Pier, Disney California Adventure)

12 **JACK-JACK'S NUM NUM COOKIES** (Pixar Pier, Disney California Adventure)

13 **PIXAR PIER FROSTY PARFAITS** (Pixar Pier, Disney California Adventure)

14 **SEÑOR BUZZ'S CALIENTE CHURROS** (Pixar Pier, Disney California Adventure)

15 **BAVARIAN PRETZELS** (Pacific Wharf, Disney California Adventure)

16 **SALLY'S SUMMER CHURROS** (Cars Land, Disney California Adventure)

Mangonada Smoothies

Hollywood Land, Disney California Adventure

· · · ✦ · · ·

This delicious and refreshing Mexican treat sure helps beat the heat on a California summer day. The mix of salty, spicy, and sweet is so satisfying. Actually, a recent study found that adding salt to a sweet treat helps release the sugar flavors and brings out even more of the sweetness!

SERVES 2

- ½ cup pineapple juice
- ½ cup guava juice
- 1 cup frozen mango chunks
- ½ cup frozen peach chunks
- 1 whole fresh banana, peeled
- 4 teaspoons chamoy sauce, divided
- ½ cup fresh chopped mango
- ½ teaspoon chili-lime seasoning

1. Combine pineapple juice, guava juice, frozen mango chunks, frozen peach chunks, and banana in a blender and blend until smooth.

2. Drizzle 1 teaspoon chamoy sauce inside walls of two drinking glasses. Divide smoothie mixture into glasses, add ¼ cup fresh mango to each cup, drizzle another 1 teaspoon chamoy sauce in each glass, and sprinkle ¼ teaspoon chili-lime seasoning on each.

Carnitas Tacos

Hollywood Land, Disney California Adventure

· · · ✦ · · ·

Tacos have been around a long time. A really, *really* long time. They were basically born out of necessity, since tools like forks and spoons were hard to come by. A tortilla was an edible plate! Now, folks can't get enough of these little meals—Disney-goers included. Originally a great way to stay full between thrilling rides at Disney California Adventure, these savory pork tacos can now fill you up at home.

SERVES 5

1 tablespoon paprika
1 teaspoon chili powder
1 teaspoon salt
2 tablespoons light brown sugar
1 tablespoon ground cinnamon
1¾ pounds boneless pork, cut into 2" chunks
1 medium yellow onion, peeled and quartered
6 medium cloves garlic, peeled and crushed
3 tablespoons shortening
2 large oranges, divided
2 large bay leaves
2 cups red and green shredded cabbage mix
1 cup medium salsa
1 cup sour cream
10 (8") flour tortillas

1. In a medium bowl, add paprika, chili powder, salt, brown sugar, and cinnamon. Stir to combine. Working with one chunk of pork at a time, roll meat in spice mix to fully coat, then place in an electric pressure cooker. Continue until all pieces are covered and pork is in a single layer in the bottom of the cooker.

2. Wedge onion and garlic between pork pieces. Place pieces of shortening evenly around top of the pork. Slice 1 orange into rounds and lay rounds evenly across pork. Place bay leaves on top and squeeze juice from second orange over pork.

3. Cover and set to "pressure cook" or "manual." Set cook time for 30 minutes.

4. Preheat broiler to high. Line a large ungreased baking sheet with parchment paper and set aside.

5. When pork is done, allow pressure cooker to naturally release pressure 10 minutes, then quick-release remaining pressure.

6. Discard bay leaves. Using tongs, transfer pork pieces to prepared baking sheet and drizzle with a few spoonfuls of the cooking liquid. Broil 5 minutes. Stir and broil 5 minutes more.

7. Divide pork, cabbage, salsa, and sour cream evenly among tortillas. Fold into tacos.

Berry Schmoozies

Hollywood Land, Disney California Adventure

• • • ✦ • • •

Schmoozies! is a little counter in Hollywood Land where you can pick up a cold blended beverage to cool off in the California sun. You may have the pleasure of meeting (and taking a photo) with your friendly neighborhood Spider-Man too! This is a rare opportunity not available in any of the Disney World parks in Florida due to licensing laws in place before Disney's acquisition of Marvel properties.

SERVES 2

½ cup pineapple juice
½ cup low-fat vanilla yogurt
½ cup unsweetened frozen blackberries
½ cup unsweetened frozen raspberries
½ cup unsweetened frozen strawberries

In a blender, add all ingredients and blend until smooth. Divide between two glasses.

Churro Toffee

Buena Vista Street, Disney California Adventure

· · · ✦ · · ·

Churro Toffee has quickly risen up the ranks as one of the most popular Disneyland treats. Unfortunately for East Coasters, this treat hasn't made its way to Walt Disney World, but now you can enjoy it anytime right at home!

YIELDS 24 TOFFEES

2 cups salted cold butter

12½ cups granulated sugar, divided

6 tablespoons light corn syrup

6 tablespoons room-temperature water

2 teaspoons vanilla extract

2 (12-ounce) bags white chocolate chips

6 tablespoons ground cinnamon

1. In a medium pot over medium heat, add butter, 2½ cups sugar, corn syrup, and water. Stir until butter is melted and mixture begins to boil, about 4 minutes.

2. Boil without stirring until mixture reaches 300°F on a candy thermometer. Remove from heat and stir in vanilla.

3. Line an ungreased baking sheet with parchment paper. Pour mixture onto center of sheet and let spread out.

4. Wait about 10 minutes for toffee to slightly cool, then use a knife to score lines into the toffee, making 24 squares.

5. Once it begins to harden, about 30 minutes, break along scored lines, then let cool completely on sheet, about 30 minutes.

6. In a medium microwave-safe bowl, add 1 bag chocolate chips. Microwave on high 30 seconds, stir, then microwave 15 seconds. Repeat microwaving in 15-second increments, stirring between each, until chocolate just barely melts.

7. Fill a large rimmed baking sheet about ½" deep with remaining 10 cups sugar and sprinkle with cinnamon. Stir. Fill a small bowl with some cinnamon sugar from sheet.

8. Use a paper towel to blot excess butter from each square. Submerge a square in melted chocolate. Place coated toffee on baking sheet of cinnamon sugar. Spoon additional cinnamon sugar from small bowl onto toffee. Repeat to coat 12 squares. Allow squares to sit on sheet until chocolate has fully hardened, about 30 minutes. Remove toffees from sugar and repeat with remaining toffee squares and second bag of chocolate chips. Store in an airtight container at room temperature up to 7 days.

Pumpkin Spice Churros

Buena Vista Street, Disney California Adventure

· · · ✦ · · ·

For Halloween at the Disneyland Resort in 2019, ten specialty churros were served, including these Pumpkin Spice Churros. You can only find them at Disneyland during the fall season, but now they can be enjoyed any time of year in your own home!

YIELDS 8 CHURROS

1 cup room-temperature water
½ cup pumpkin purée
2 tablespoons plus 4 cups vegetable oil, divided
1 teaspoon vanilla extract
1¾ cups all-purpose flour
3 tablespoons plus ½ cup granulated sugar, divided
1 teaspoon pumpkin pie spice
½ teaspoon salt
1 teaspoon ground cinnamon

1. Line an ungreased baking sheet with parchment paper.

2. In a large bowl, whisk together water, pumpkin purée, 2 tablespoons oil, and vanilla. Add flour, 3 tablespoons sugar, pumpkin pie spice, and salt. Mix well by hand.

3. Scoop dough into a piping bag fitted with a large star tip. Chill bag in refrigerator 1 hour.

4. Pipe dough into 6" lines onto prepared baking sheet. Place sheet in freezer to set 15 minutes.

5. In a large pot over medium-high heat, add remaining 4 cups oil to reach a depth of about 3". Heat until oil reaches 375°F. Line a large plate with paper towels and set aside.

6. In a long, shallow pan, mix remaining ½ cup sugar and cinnamon. Set aside.

7. Slide one churro into hot oil. Fry until golden brown, about 2 minutes. Remove from oil with tongs and place directly into cinnamon sugar. Turn to coat thoroughly and transfer to lined plate to cool. Repeat with remaining churros.

MIX IT UP

This churro is served in the parks with a side of cream cheese frosting. To make your own, just combine 4 ounces softened cream cheese with ¼ cup softened salted butter, 2 cups confectioners' sugar, and 1 tablespoon heavy cream. Whisk until smooth. Yummy!

Campfire Chili

Grizzly Peak, Disney California Adventure

· · · ✦ · · ·

Grizzly River Run may seem like a harrowing adventure, but the longest drop is only 22 feet—though it may not be the drop you need to worry about, because guests tend to leave Grizzly River Run soaked from head to foot! Whether spending the day gliding along the river or curled up at home, warm up your insides with a hot cup of Campfire Chili. You can't go wrong with this simple yet hearty comfort food, a favorite at Grizzly Peak's Smokejumpers Grill.

SERVES 10

1 tablespoon vegetable oil
1 medium yellow onion, peeled and diced
2 teaspoons minced garlic
1 pound ground beef
3 (15-ounce) cans black beans, including juices
2 (14.5-ounce) cans crushed tomatoes, including juices
1 tablespoon dried oregano
1 tablespoon dried basil
2 tablespoons ground cumin
1 tablespoon curry powder
1 tablespoon salt
1 teaspoon ground black pepper
1 tablespoon red wine vinegar

1. In a large pot over medium heat, add oil, onion, and garlic. Cook until onion is translucent, about 3 minutes. Add ground beef and stir until browned, about 6 minutes.

2. Add remaining ingredients. Stir, then reduce heat to low and simmer uncovered 1 hour. Leftovers can be kept in an airtight container in the refrigerator for up to 1 week.

S'mores

Grizzly Peak, Disney California Adventure

· · · ✦ · · ·

Walt Disney believed in the sanctity of the outdoors. According to the Disneyland Resort News site, he said, "Physical America—the land itself—should be as dear to us all as our political heritage and our treasured way of life. Its preservation and the wise conservation of its renewable resources concerns every man, woman, and child whose possession it is." Now you can bring the great outdoors to your own kitchen with these S'mores!

YIELDS 6 S'MORES

½ cup semisweet chocolate chips
6 graham crackers, halved
6 extra-large marshmallows
3 (4-ounce) white chocolate candy bars

1. Grease a large plate lightly with nonstick cooking spray and set aside.

2. In a medium microwave-safe bowl, add chocolate chips. Microwave on high 15 seconds, stir, then microwave 15 seconds. Repeat microwaving in 15-second increments, stirring between each, until chocolate just barely melts.

3. Use a knife or offset spatula to spread a thin layer of melted chocolate on the front, back, and sides of each graham cracker square. Lay on greased plate and chill in the freezer 30 minutes.

4. Skewer one marshmallow and toast to your desired doneness using a stove flame or kitchen torch. Repeat with remaining marshmallows.

5. Place 1 toasted marshmallow between 2 chocolate-coated graham crackers. Place a piece of white chocolate candy bar on top. Repeat with remaining ingredients.

Cobbler Shakes

Grizzly Peak, Disney California Adventure

· · · ✦ · · ·

This yummy treat is sold at Smokejumpers Grill, which pays homage to the men and women who fight the California wildfires. Smoke jumpers are an elite group of firefighters who parachute directly into a fire zone and fight the fire from the inside. Made with vanilla and apple pie flavors, the Cobbler Shake at Smokejumpers Grill is a filling treat that satisfies firefighters and Disney-goers alike.

SERVES 4

1 cup whole milk
1 cup apple juice
4 cups vanilla ice cream
1 teaspoon ground cinnamon
¼ teaspoon ground nutmeg
¼ teaspoon ground allspice

In a blender, add all ingredients. Blend until combined. Divide among four tall drinking glasses.

Corn Dogs

Paradise Gardens Park, Disney California Adventure

· · · ✦ · · ·

Sitting and watching Goofy's Sky School is great fun while enjoying a Corn Dog Castle Original Corn Dog. For a similar experience at home, search on the Internet for "Disney POV Rides" and virtually hop on your favorite attractions—without having to leave your delicious treat behind! These filling Corn Dogs make a perfect snack, side, or even entrée the whole family will love.

SERVES 8

4 cups vegetable oil for frying
1 cup yellow cornmeal
1 cup all-purpose flour
½ cup granulated sugar
½ teaspoon salt
½ teaspoon ground black pepper
4 teaspoons baking powder
1¼ cups whole milk
1 large egg
8 beef hot dogs

1. In a large, heavy-bottomed pot over medium-high heat, add vegetable oil. It should measure to a depth of about 3". Heat until oil reaches 350°F. Line a large plate with paper towels and set aside.

2. In a large bowl, mix together cornmeal, flour, sugar, salt, pepper, and baking powder. Add milk and egg and whisk together well.

3. Pour batter into a tall drinking glass ¾ full and set aside.

4. Insert Popsicle sticks into hot dogs and wipe each hot dog with a paper towel to help batter stick.

5. Dip one hot dog into batter in glass. Carefully remove and lower immediately into hot oil.

6. Fry until deep golden brown, about 3 minutes, turning frequently. Transfer to lined plate. Repeat with remaining hot dogs. Leftover batter can be kept in a sealed container in the refrigerator up to 5 days.

Chicken Drumsticks

Pixar Pier, Disney California Adventure

· · · ✦ · · ·

Poultry Palace was originally seen in the Pixar short film *Small Fry*, a spin-off of the Toy Story franchise, and included fan favorites like Woody and Buzz. Now the chicken shop has made cameo appearances in several other Pixar films, including *Onward*. This lovable-looking, meal box–shaped establishment started gracing Pixar Pier in 2018, with Chicken Drumsticks offering a protein-packed snack or entrée to tide over guests.

SERVES 6

½ cup cold salted butter
¼ cup all-purpose flour
½ cup yellow cornmeal
2 teaspoons salt
2 teaspoons paprika
1 teaspoon ground dried sage
½ teaspoon ground black pepper
6 (4-ounce) skin-on chicken drumsticks

1. Place butter in a 9" × 13" baking pan and put pan into oven. Preheat oven to 450°F.

2. In a large resealable plastic bag, add flour, cornmeal, salt, paprika, sage, and pepper. Close bag and shake to combine.

3. Once oven is heated, carefully remove pan.

4. Place one drumstick into seasoning bag and shake to coat. Then place drumstick into buttered pan. Repeat with remaining drumsticks. Carefully pat leftover seasoning from bag onto drumsticks.

5. Bake 20 minutes. Flip drumsticks and bake 20 minutes more, or until thermometer inserted in center reaches 165°F. Serve immediately.

MIX IT UP

Poultry Palace serves their Chicken Drumsticks with coleslaw, and you can too! Mix together ¾ cup mayonnaise, 3 tablespoons apple cider vinegar, 1 tablespoon Dijon mustard, ½ teaspoon salt, and ½ teaspoon ground black pepper. Drizzle over 1 bag (about 8 cups) shredded coleslaw mix. This creates a tangy side that pairs beautifully with the drumsticks!

Chili-Lime Corn on the Cob

Pixar Pier, Disney California Adventure

Nothing says warm weather like a delicious bite of corn on the cob—whether in California, or anywhere across the US. And adding zesty flavors takes this classic snack to the next level. You can make this recipe with ready-made chili-lime seasoning or make your own with fresh lime juice, chili powder, and dried cilantro. Either way is delicious!

SERVES 6

6 medium ears corn, shucked
½ cup salted butter, softened
1 tablespoon chili-lime seasoning

1. Preheat grill to medium.

2. Lay out six pieces of aluminum foil and place 1 cob on each. Rub butter all over corn and season with chili-lime seasoning.

3. Wrap corn in foil and place on grill. Grill 7 minutes, flip, and grill 7 minutes more, until corn is bright and firm.

Jack-Jack's Num Num Cookies

Pixar Pier, Disney California Adventure

· · · ✦ · · ·

When all you want after a long day of waiting in lines is a sweet treat, Pixar Pier has you covered! These monstrously thick cookies originated with the hit movie *Incredibles 2*, when Bob Parr has to use "Cookie Num Nums" to lure his baby, Jack-Jack, out of different dimensions. Serve these rich and delicious cookies with a side of milk.

SERVES 3

3 tablespoons unsalted butter, softened
3 tablespoons vegetable shortening
¼ cup light brown sugar
¼ cup granulated sugar
½ teaspoon vanilla extract
1 large egg
¾ cup all-purpose flour
½ teaspoon baking soda
½ teaspoon salt
1 cup milk chocolate chunks, divided

1. Preheat oven to 375°F. Line three (4") ramekins with parchment paper and set aside.

2. In the bowl of a stand mixer, add butter and shortening. Using the flat beater attachment, cream together well. Add brown sugar and granulated sugar, and beat 2 minutes. Mix in vanilla and egg, then mix in flour, baking soda, and salt. Stir in ¾ cup chocolate chunks.

3. Pack each ramekin with about ½" cookie dough, top dough with remaining ¼ cup chocolate chunks, and bake 15 minutes.

4. Allow to cool completely, about 15 minutes, before removing from ramekins.

DID YOU KNOW?

The character Jack-Jack displays eleven different powers in the movie Incredibles 2. *These include bursting into flames, invisibility, laser vision, teleportation, and turning into a demon. And you thought normal babies were hard to handle!*

Pixar Pier Frosty Parfaits

Pixar Pier, Disney California Adventure

· · · ✦ · · ·

These adorable frosted treats on Pixar Pier pay homage to the lovable yeti seen in the Pixar film *Monsters, Inc.* We meet him when Mike and Sulley are banished to the Himalayas for disobeying rules. The yeti is serving "yellow snow" in the movie, which everyone knows you shouldn't eat! Luckily, these cute parfaits have lots of "yellow snow" that your whole family can enjoy. Blue raspberry ice treats can typically be found in the Popsicle section of your grocery store.

SERVES 4

4 cups lemon sorbet
2 cups blue raspberry ice treats, mashed
4 maraschino cherries

In a parfait glass, layer ½-cup scoop lemon sorbet, ½ cup blue raspberry slush, and another ½-cup scoop of lemon sorbet. Add a cherry on top. Repeat with remaining ingredients.

Señor Buzz's Caliente Churros

Pixar Pier, Disney California Adventure

· · · ✦ · · ·

As part of Disney California Adventure's Pixar transformations in 2018, Disney introduced this new churro variety, which adds a spicy element to the classic treat. And if you're a mild-palate person, don't fear: The dough and granulated sugar balance the "caliente" quality to keep it from being overpowering.

SERVES 12

1 cup Red Hots cinnamon candies
¼ cup granulated sugar
5 drops red gel food coloring
12 Churros (see recipe in Chapter 3)

1. In a food processor, add Red Hots and process until they are a fine powder. Add sugar and red food coloring to Red Hots, processing until they are a bold, bright red color.

2. Transfer Red Hots mixture to a large plate. Roll still-hot Churros in the red dust until totally covered. Serve immediately.

Bavarian Pretzels

Pacific Wharf, Disney California Adventure

· · · ✦ · · ·

Pacific Wharf is the only land at the entire Disneyland Resort with no major attractions. It is simply a place to rest, relax, and grab a bite to eat. You can tour the Boudin Bakery sourdough bread factory (it ends with a free sample of bread!), and stop for lunch at Pacific Wharf, where there is something for everyone in your vacation party. These Bavarian Pretzels are great at filling up hungry tummies, whether at Disney or in your own home.

YIELDS 6 PRETZELS

9 cups plus 1 tablespoon warm water (110°F), divided
1 (¼-ounce) packet active dry yeast
½ teaspoon salt
4½ cups all-purpose flour
½ cup baking soda
1 large egg
2 tablespoons kosher salt

1. In the bowl of a stand mixer, pour ¼ cup warm water. Sprinkle yeast on top of water. Let sit 5 minutes.

2. Add 1¼ cups warm water, salt, and flour to yeast mixture. Using the flat beater attachment, beat on low until mixture starts to form a ball. Switch to dough hook attachment and knead 5 minutes. If dough appears too dry and isn't coming together, add 1 extra tablespoon water at a time until dough comes together.

3. Remove dough from mixer and knead by hand 2 minutes or until ball is soft and elastic.

4. Preheat oven to 400°F. Line an ungreased baking sheet with parchment paper and set aside.

5. Cut dough into six equal parts. Working with one piece at a time, hold one end of a piece in one hand and use the other hand to roll the dough with your heel and palm. Keep switching hands until the rope is about 30" long and ⅓" wide. Repeat with remaining dough.

(continued) ▶

6. Hold one strand up in a *U* shape. Cross the top pieces over one another and twist. Bring them back down toward you and press into the bottom of the *U*. Repeat with remaining dough strands. Place on prepared baking sheet and allow to rest 10 minutes.

7. Fill a large pot with 7½ cups water and bring to a boil over high heat. Once boiling, add baking soda and stir.

8. Use a slotted spoon to slide 1 pretzel into baking soda bath and poach 15 seconds. Remove to prepared baking sheet. Repeat with remaining pretzels.

9. In a small bowl, beat egg and remaining 1 tablespoon water together. Brush onto each pretzel. Sprinkle kosher salt on top of pretzels.

10. Bake pretzels until deep golden brown, about 18 minutes. Serve immediately or store in an airtight container up to 2 days.

Sally's Summer Churros

Cars Land, Disney California Adventure

· · · ✦ · · ·

Seasonal churros are a favorite in Disney Parks—in fact, some guests come just to try the new flavors sold each month! This summer variation has a bright and fresh taste, with strawberries and cream cheese playing off one another to create a fruity, creamy profile. And if you want to make these in the middle of winter, who's to stop you? Live your best summer churro life!

YIELDS 12 CHURROS

For Strawberry Syrup

1 pound frozen strawberries
1 cup granulated sugar
1 tablespoon lemon juice

1. In a medium saucepan over medium heat, add strawberries, sugar, and lemon juice. Bring to a boil and cook 3 minutes, stirring continuously and mashing down the strawberries as they get soft. Remove from heat. Allow to cool slightly, about 10 minutes.

2. In a blender, pour strawberry mixture and blend until smooth. Let cool about 10 minutes, then scoop into a piping bag.

(continued) ▶

For Cream Cheese Frosting

¼ cup salted butter, softened
2 cups confectioners' sugar
4 ounces cream cheese,
  softened
1 tablespoon heavy cream
12 Churros (see recipe in
  Chapter 3)

1. In the bowl of a stand mixer, add butter, confectioners' sugar, cream cheese, and heavy cream. Using the flat beater attachment, beat on high until well combined. Scoop frosting into a separate piping bag.

2. Lay out still-warm Churros. Cut tips off piping bags and pipe squiggles of Cream Cheese Frosting over each Churro, followed by squiggles of Strawberry Syrup. Serve immediately.

DID YOU KNOW?

Fresh or frozen strawberries can be used for this recipe. If you have some strawberries that are nearing the end of their life, you can cook them into this syrup and it will last up to a week in the refrigerator. It isn't just delicious on Churros; try using on pancakes or waffles!

Standard US/Metric Measurement Conversions

VOLUME CONVERSIONS	
US Volume Measure	**Metric Equivalent**
⅛ teaspoon	0.5 milliliter
¼ teaspoon	1 milliliter
½ teaspoon	2 milliliters
1 teaspoon	5 milliliters
½ tablespoon	7 milliliters
1 tablespoon (3 teaspoons)	15 milliliters
2 tablespoons (1 fluid ounce)	30 milliliters
¼ cup (4 tablespoons)	60 milliliters
⅓ cup	90 milliliters
½ cup (4 fluid ounces)	125 milliliters
⅔ cup	160 milliliters
¾ cup (6 fluid ounces)	180 milliliters
1 cup (16 tablespoons)	250 milliliters
1 pint (2 cups)	500 milliliters
1 quart (4 cups)	1 liter (about)
WEIGHT CONVERSIONS	
US Weight Measure	**Metric Equivalent**
½ ounce	15 grams
1 ounce	30 grams
2 ounces	60 grams
3 ounces	85 grams
¼ pound (4 ounces)	115 grams
½ pound (8 ounces)	225 grams
¾ pound (12 ounces)	340 grams
1 pound (16 ounces)	454 grams

OVEN TEMPERATURE CONVERSIONS

Degrees Fahrenheit	Degrees Celsius
200 degrees F	95 degrees C
250 degrees F	120 degrees C
275 degrees F	135 degrees C
300 degrees F	150 degrees C
325 degrees F	160 degrees C
350 degrees F	180 degrees C
375 degrees F	190 degrees C
400 degrees F	205 degrees C
425 degrees F	220 degrees C
450 degrees F	230 degrees C

BAKING PAN SIZES

American	Metric
8 × 1½ inch round baking pan	20 × 4 cm cake tin
9 × 1½ inch round baking pan	23 × 3.5 cm cake tin
11 × 7 × 1½ inch baking pan	28 × 18 × 4 cm baking tin
13 × 9 × 2 inch baking pan	30 × 20 × 5 cm baking tin
2 quart rectangular baking dish	30 × 20 × 3 cm baking tin
15 × 10 × 2 inch baking pan	30 × 25 × 2 cm baking tin (Swiss roll tin)
9 inch pie plate	22 × 4 or 23 × 4 cm pie plate
7 or 8 inch springform pan	18 or 20 cm springform or loose bottom cake tin
9 × 5 × 3 inch loaf pan	23 × 13 × 7 cm or 2 lb narrow loaf or pâté tin
1½ quart casserole	1.5 liter casserole
2 quart casserole	2 liter casserole

Index

A

Adventureland, Disneyland
Bengal Beef Skewers, 60
Hummus Trio, 63–64
Jungle Juleps, 61
Pork Belly Skewers, 65
Safari Skewers, 66
Tiger Tail Breadsticks, 62
Adventureland, Magic Kingdom
Cheeseburger Steamed Rolls, 106
Dole Whip, 109
Pineapple Upside Down Cake, 110
Pizza Spring Rolls, 107
Africa, Disney's Animal Kingdom
Haystacks, 179
Mickey Waffles, 178
Animal Kingdom. *See* Disney's Animal Kingdom
Apple(s)
Candy Apples, 151
Caramel Apples, 86
Cobbler Shakes, 213
Asia, Disney's Animal Kingdom, Mr. Kamal's Seasoned Fries, 189
Asparagus, in Safari Skewers, 66

B

Bacon. *See* Pork
Baked Lobster Macaroni & Cheese, 199
Baked Macaroni & Cheese with Pulled Pork, 196–98
Baking sheets, 34
Baklava, 144–45

Bananas
Fresh Fruit Waffle Sandwiches, 93
Frozen Chocolate-Covered Bananas, 173
Bavarian Cheesecake, 134
Bavarian Pretzels, 223–24
Beans
Campfire Chili, 211
Hummus Trio, 63–64
Beef
Bengal Beef Skewers, 60
Campfire Chili, 211
Cheeseburger Steamed Pods, 182–83
Cheeseburger Steamed Rolls, 106
Beignets, 67–69
Bengal Beef Skewers, 60
Berries
Berry Schmoozies, 208
Blueberry Cream Cheese Mousse, 185–87
Fresh Fruit Waffle Sandwiches, 93
Lemon-Blueberry Lunch Box Tarts, 162
Pixar Pier Frosty Parfaits, 221
Raspberry Rose Mickey Macarons, 54–56
Sally's Summer Churros, 225–26
Strawberry Kakigōri, 136
Strawberry Syrup, 225
Tarte aux Fraises, 124–26
Blenders, 34, 38
Blue Milk, 165
Breads and such. *See also* Sandwiches
about: muffin pans, 39
Croissant Doughnuts, 117
Fritters, 70
Gaston's Giant Cinnamon Rolls, 99–100
School Bread, 127
Tiger Tail Breadsticks, 62

Brownie Bites, 79
Buena Vista Street, Disney California
  Adventure
    Churro Toffee, 209
    Pumpkin Spice Churros, 210
Butterfinger Cupcakes, 154–55
Butterscotch Topping, 100

C

Cake pans, 35
Cakes. *See* Cookies, cakes, and cupcakes
Candy Apples, 151
Caramel
    Caramel Apples, 86
    Caramel Pecan Bars, 133
    Caramel Popcorn, 131
    Chocolate-Caramel Pineapple Spears, 132
Cars Land, Disney California Adventure,
  Sally's Summer Churros, 225–26
Carnitas Tacos, 206–7
Carrot Cake Cookies, 153
Cheese. *See also* Macaroni & cheese
    Bavarian Cheesecake, 134
    Blueberry Cream Cheese Mousse, 185–87
    Cheeseburger Steamed Pods, 182–83
    Cheeseburger Steamed Rolls, 106
    Cream Cheese Frosting, 100, 153, 226
    French Fries with Pulled Pork and Cheese,
      195
    Pizza Spring Rolls, 107
    Pongu Lumpia, 188
    Pretzels with Cream Cheese Filling, 156–57
Cheshire Cat Tails, 94–95
Chicken and turkey
    Chicken Drumsticks, 216
    Loaded Buffalo Chicken Tots, 104–5
    Sweet-and-Spicy Chicken Waffle
      Sandwiches, 89–90
    Turkey Legs, 103
Chickpeas, Hummus Trio, 63–64
Chili, 211
Chili-Lime Corn on the Cob, 217

Chocolate
    Brownie Bites, 79
    Butterfinger Cupcakes, 154–55
    Cheshire Cat Tails, 94–95
    Chocolate-Caramel Pineapple Spears, 132
    Chocolate-Hazelnut Lunch Box Tarts, 161
    Cookies and Cream Mickey Cupcakes,
      57–59
    Frozen Chocolate-Covered Bananas, 173
    The Grey Stuff, 97
    Jack-Jack's Num Num Cookies, 218–19
    Mickey Ice Cream Bars, 194
    Mickey Ice Cream Sandwiches, 193
    S'mores, 212
    Stracciatella Gelato, 143
Chocolate, white
    Blueberry Cream Cheese Mousse, 185–87
    Churro Toffee, 209
    Matterhorn Macaroons, 78
    S'mores, 212
Churros, 53
    Churro Funnel Cake, 75
    Churro Toffee, 209
    Pumpkin Spice Churros, 210
    Sally's Summer Churros, 225–26
    Señor Buzz's Caliente Churros, 222
Cinnamon rolls, Gaston's giant, 99–100
Citrus
    Frozen Lemonade, 190–91
    Gold Port Galley Lemonade, 74
    Green Milk, 163–64
    Jungle Juleps, 61
    Lemon-Blueberry Lunch Box Tarts, 162
    Night Blossoms, 180–81
    Orange Cream, 129
Clam Chowder, 71
Cobbler Shakes, 213
Coconut
    Cocco Gelato, 141–42
    Coconut Popsicles, 140
    Matterhorn Macaroons, 78
College Program, Disney, 24
Cookies, cakes, and cupcakes

Brownie Bites, 79
Buttercream Frosting, 154
Butterfinger Cupcakes, 154–55
Carrot Cake Cookies, 153
Churro Funnel Cake, 75
Cookies and Cream Mickey Cupcakes, 57–59
Funnel Cake, 91
The Grey Stuff Gâteau, 76–77
Jack-Jack's Num Num Cookies, 218–19
Macaron Ice Cream Sandwiches, 118
Matterhorn Macaroons, 78
Mickey Sugar Cookies, 85
Pineapple Upside Down Cake, 110
Raspberry Rose Mickey Macarons, 54–56
Cooking essentials, 33–45
about: overview of, 33
baking sheets, 34
blender, 34
cake pans, 35
cookie cutters, 35
cookie scoop, 35
cooling rack, 36
electric pressure cooker, 36
food coloring, 36
food processor, 37
grill or grill pan, 37
ice cream machine, 37–38
immersion blender, 38
muffin pans, 38
paper grocery bags, 39
parchment paper, 39
piping bags, 39–40
popsicle molds and sticks, 40
pots and pans, 41
ramekins, 41
rolling pin, 41
shaved ice maker, 42
sieve/sifter, 42
springform pan, 43
stand mixer, 43
steamer basket, 44
thermometers, 44

wooden skewers, 45
Corn and popcorn
Caramel Popcorn, 131
Chili-Lime Corn on the Cob, 217
Maple Popcorn, 111
Outpost Popcorn Mix (Spicy Popcorn and Sweet Popcorn), 166–67
Perfect Popcorn, 152
Corn Dog Nuggets, 88
Corn Dogs, 215
Crème Pâtissière, 124–26
Crêpes, 123
Critter Country, Disneyland
Churro Funnel Cake, 75
Gold Port Galley Lemonade, 74
Croissant Doughnuts, 117
Croque Glacé, 119–20
Cupcakes. *See* Cookies, cakes, and cupcakes

D

Desserts and sweet snacks. *See also* Breads and such; Churros; Cookies, cakes, and cupcakes; Ice cream and frozen treats; Waffles
about: baking pans for, 34, 35; cookie cutters/scoops for, 35; cooling rack for, 36; piping bags and tips, 39–40
Baklava, 144–45
Bavarian Cheesecake, 134
Beignets, 67–69
Blueberry Cream Cheese Mousse, 185–87
Candy Apples, 151
Caramel Apples, 86
Caramel Pecan Bars, 133
Caramel Popcorn, 131
Cheshire Cat Tails, 94–95
Chocolate-Caramel Pineapple Spears, 132
Chocolate-Hazelnut Lunch Box Tarts, 161
Crème Pâtissière, 124–26
Crêpes, 123
Croissant Doughnuts, 117
Dole Whip, 109
Gaston's Giant Cinnamon Rolls, 99–100

231

The Grey Stuff, 97
Haystacks, 179
Lemon-Blueberry Lunch Box Tarts, 162
Mangonada Smoothies, 205
Maple Popcorn, 111
Napoleons, 121–22
Perfect Popcorn, 152
Pongu Lumpia, 188
Pretzels with Cream Cheese Filling, 156–57
School Bread, 127
Tarte aux Fraises, 124–26
Troll Horns, 128–29
Discovery Island, Disney's Animal Kingdom
Baked Lobster Macaroni & Cheese, 199
Baked Macaroni & Cheese with Pulled Pork, 196–98
French Fries with Pulled Pork and Cheese, 195
Frozen Lemonade, 190–91
Mickey Ice Cream Bars, 194
Mickey Ice Cream Sandwiches, 193
Disney. *See also specific Disney Parks*
about: overview of this book and, 16–17, 19, 21
your Disney cuisine, 31
Disney California Adventure, 201–26
about: Asian cuisine, 30; big-screen-inspired treats, 30; Mexican/Hispanic roots focus, 29; Northern California specialties (wine and sourdough bread), 30; overview of park foods and layout, 201–3
Bavarian Pretzels, 223–24
Berry Schmoozies, 208
Campfire Chili, 211
Carnitas Tacos, 206–7
Chicken Drumsticks, 216
Chili-Lime Corn on the Cob, 217
Churro Toffee, 209
Cobbler Shakes, 213
Corn Dogs, 215
Jack-Jack's Num Num Cookies, 218–19
Mangonada Smoothies, 205

Pixar Pier Frosty Parfaits, 221
Pumpkin Spice Churros, 210
Sally's Summer Churros, 225–26
Señor Buzz's Caliente Churros, 222
S'mores, 212
Disney College Program, 24
Disneyland, 49–79
about: contracted and sponsored foods at, 22–23; food culture at, 22–23; Magic Kingdom compared to, 23–24; new, fun treats in the 1950s, 23; opening of, 22; overview of park foods and layout, 49–51
Beignets, 67–69
Bengal Beef Skewers, 60
Brownie Bites, 79
Churro Funnel Cake, 75
Churros, 53
Clam Chowder, 71
Cookies and Cream Mickey Cupcakes, 57–59
Fritters, 70
Gold Port Galley Lemonade, 74
The Grey Stuff Gâteau, 76–77
Hummus Trio, 63–64
Jungle Juleps, 61
Matterhorn Macaroons, 78
Mint Juleps, 72–73
Pork Belly Skewers, 65
Raspberry Rose Mickey Macarons, 54–56
Safari Skewers, 66
Tiger Tail Breadsticks, 62
Disney's Animal Kingdom, 175–99
about: immersive food experience, 28–29; overview of park foods and layout, 175–77; Pandora—The World of Avatar food challenges, 29; uniquenesses of, 28
Baked Lobster Macaroni & Cheese, 199
Baked Macaroni & Cheese with Pulled Pork, 196–98
Blueberry Cream Cheese Mousse, 185–87
Cheeseburger Steamed Pods, 182–83
French Fries with Pulled Pork and Cheese, 195

Frozen Lemonade, 190–91
Haystacks, 179
Mickey Ice Cream Bars, 194
Mickey Ice Cream Sandwiches, 193
Mickey Waffles, 178
Mr. Kamal's Seasoned Fries, 189
Night Blossoms, 180–81
Pongu Lumpia, 188
Disney's Hollywood Studios, 147–73
about: eclectic food culture, 26–27; overview of park foods and layout, 147–73; table service focus, 27; Toy Story Land and Star Wars: Galaxy's Edge impact, 27–28
Blue Milk, 165
Butterfinger Cupcakes, 154–55
Candy Apples, 151
Carrot Cake Cookies, 153
Chocolate-Hazelnut Lunch Box Tarts, 161
Frozen Chocolate-Covered Bananas, 173
Green Milk, 163–64
Lemon-Blueberry Lunch Box Tarts, 162
Mickey Pretzels, 158–60
Outpost Popcorn Mix (Spicy Popcorn and Sweet Popcorn), 166–67
Peanut Butter and Jelly Milk Shakes, 171
Perfect Popcorn, 152
Pretzels with Cream Cheese Filling, 156–57
Ronto Wraps, 169–70
Dole Whip, 109
Doughnuts, croissant, 117
Drinks. *See also* Ice cream and frozen treats
Berry Schmoozies, 208
Blue Milk, 165
Cobbler Shakes, 213
Gold Port Galley Lemonade, 74
Green Milk, 163–64
Jungle Juleps, 61
LeFou's Brew, 96
Mangonada Smoothies, 205
Mint Juleps, 72–73

Mint Syrup for, 72
Night Blossoms, 180–81
Peanut Butter and Jelly Milk Shakes, 171
Peter Pan Floats, 101

E

Echo Lake, Disney's Hollywood Studios
Frozen Chocolate-Covered Bananas, 173
Peanut Butter and Jelly Milk Shakes, 171
Eggs. *See also* Waffles
Crêpes, 123
Fritters, 70
Ronto Wraps, 169–70
Electric pressure cooker, 36
EPCOT, 113–45
about: annual festivals, 25–26; as culinary mecca, 25; dedication to food production sustainability, 26; "drinking around the world," 25; overview of park foods and layout, 113–45
Baklava, 144–45
Bavarian Cheesecake, 134
Caramel Pecan Bars, 133
Caramel Popcorn, 131
Chocolate-Caramel Pineapple Spears, 132
Cocco Gelato, 141–42
Coconut Popsicles, 140
Crêpes, 123
Croissant Doughnuts, 117
Croque Glacé, 119–20
Macaron Ice Cream Sandwiches, 118
Mango Popsicles, 139
Melon Kakigōri, 137
Napoleons, 121–22
School Bread, 127
Stracciatella Gelato, 143
Strawberry Kakigōri, 136
Tarte aux Fraises, 124–26
Troll Horns, 128–29

F

Fantasyland, Disneyland
 The Grey Stuff Gâteau, 76–77
 Matterhorn Macaroons, 78
Fantasyland, Magic Kingdom
 Cheshire Cat Tails, 94–95
 Gaston's Giant Cinnamon Rolls, 99–100
 The Grey Stuff, 97
 LeFou's Brew, 96
 Loaded Buffalo Chicken Tots, 104–5
 Peter Pan Floats, 101
 Tomato Basil Soup, 102
 Turkey Legs, 103
Festivals, annual, 25–26
Food coloring, 37
Food processor, 37
France, EPCOT
 Crêpes, 123
 Croque Glacé, 119–20
 Macaron Ice Cream Sandwiches, 118
 Napoleons, 121–22
 Tarte aux Fraises, 124–26
French Fries with Pulled Pork and Cheese, 195
Fresh Fruit Waffle Sandwiches, 93
Fries, 189, 195
Fritters, 70
Frontierland, Magic Kingdom, Maple Popcorn, 111
Frozen treats. *See* Ice cream and frozen treats
Funnel Cake, 91
Funnel Cake, Churro, 75
Future World, EPCOT, Croissant Doughnuts, 117

G

Gaston's Giant Cinnamon Rolls, 99–100
Gelato, stracciatella, 143
Germany, EPCOT
 Bavarian Cheesecake, 134
 Caramel Pecan Bars, 133

 Caramel Popcorn, 131
 Chocolate-Caramel Pineapple Spears, 132
Gold Port Galley Lemonade, 74
Green Milk, 163–64
The Grey Stuff, 97
The Grey Stuff Gâteau, 76–77
Grill or grill pan, 37
Grizzly Peak, Disney California Adventure
 Campfire Chili, 211
 Cobbler Shakes, 213
 S'mores, 212
Grocery bags, paper, 39

H

Haystacks, 179
Hollywood Boulevard, Disney's Hollywood Studios
 Butterfinger Cupcakes, 154–55
 Carrot Cake Cookies, 153
Hollywood Land, Disney California Adventure
 Berry Schmoozies, 208
 Carnitas Tacos, 206–7
 Mangonada Smoothies, 205
Hot dogs
 Bacon Macaroni & Cheese Hot Dogs, 87
 Corn Dog Nuggets, 88
 Corn Dogs, 215
Hummus Trio, 63–64

I

Ice cream and frozen treats
 about: ice cream machine for, 37–38; popsicle molds and sticks, 40; shaved ice maker for, 42
 Cobbler Shakes, 213
 Cocco Gelato, 141–42
 Coconut Popsicles, 140
 Croque Glacé, 119–20
 Frozen Chocolate-Covered Bananas, 173
 Frozen Lemonade, 190–91

Mango Popsicles, 139
Melon Kakigōri, 137
Mickey Ice Cream Bars, 194
Mickey Ice Cream Sandwiches, 193
Peanut Butter and Jelly Milk Shakes, 171
Peter Pan Floats, 101
Pixar Pier Frosty Parfaits, 221
Stracciatella Gelato, 143
Strawberry Kakigōri, 136
Ice cream machine, 37–38
Immersion blender, 38
An Incredible Celebration, Disney's Hollywood Studios
Mickey Pretzels, 158–60
Pretzels with Cream Cheese Filling, 156–57
Italy, EPCOT
Cocco Gelato, 141–42
Stracciatella Gelato, 143

J

Jack-Jack's Num Num Cookies, 218–19
Japan, EPCOT
Melon Kakigōri, 137
Strawberry Kakigōri, 136
Jungle Juleps, 61

L

LeFou's Brew, 96
Lemon. *See* Citrus
Liberty Square, Magic Kingdom
Fresh Fruit Waffle Sandwiches, 93
Funnel Cake, 91
Sweet-and-Spicy Chicken Waffle Sandwiches, 89–90
Loaded Buffalo Chicken Tots, 104–5

M

Macaroni & cheese
Bacon Macaroni & Cheese Hot Dogs, 87
Baked Lobster Macaroni & Cheese, 199

Baked Macaroni & Cheese with Pulled Pork, 196–98
Macarons. *See* Cookies, cakes, and cupcakes
Magic Kingdom, 81–111
about: compared to Disneyland, 23–24; contracted and sponsored foods at, 24; Disney College Program invention, 24; efficiency of, 25; overview of park foods and layout, 81–83; underground tunnels for transporting food, 24
Bacon Macaroni & Cheese Hot Dogs, 87
Caramel Apples, 86
Cheeseburger Steamed Rolls, 106
Cheshire Cat Tails, 94–95
Corn Dog Nuggets, 88
Dole Whip, 109
Fresh Fruit Waffle Sandwiches, 93
Funnel Cake, 91
Gaston's Giant Cinnamon Rolls, 99–100
The Grey Stuff, 97
LeFou's Brew, 96
Loaded Buffalo Chicken Tots, 104–5
Maple Popcorn, 111
Mickey Sugar Cookies, 85
Peter Pan Floats, 101
Pineapple Upside Down Cake, 110
Pizza Spring Rolls, 107
Sweet-and-Spicy Chicken Waffle Sandwiches, 89–90
Tomato Basil Soup, 102
Turkey Legs, 103
Main dishes. *See* Savory snacks and main dishes
Main Street, U.S.A., Disneyland
Churros, 53
Cookies and Cream Mickey Cupcakes, 57–59
Raspberry Rose Mickey Macarons, 54–56
Main Street, U.S.A., Magic Kingdom
Bacon Macaroni & Cheese Hot Dogs, 87
Caramel Apples, 86
Corn Dog Nuggets, 88
Mickey Sugar Cookies, 85

Mangonada Smoothies, 205
Mango Popsicles, 139
Maple Popcorn, 111
Marshmallows
    Haystacks, 179
    S'mores, 212
Matterhorn Macaroons, 78
Measurement conversions, 227
Melon Kakigōri, 137
Mexico, EPCOT
    Coconut Popsicles, 140
    Mango Popsicles, 139
Mickey Ice Cream Bars, 194
Mickey Ice Cream Sandwiches, 193
Mickey Pretzels, 158–60
Mickey Sugar Cookies, 85
Mickey Waffles, 178
Mint Juleps, 72–73
Mint Syrup, 72
Mixer, stand, 43
Morocco, EPCOT, Baklava, 144–45
Mr. Kamal's Seasoned Fries, 189
Muffins. *See* Breads and such

N

Napoleons, 121–22
New Orleans Square, Disneyland
    Beignets, 67–69
    Clam Chowder, 71
    Fritters, 70
    Mint Juleps, 72–73
Night Blossoms, 180–81
Norway, EPCOT
    School Bread, 127
    Troll Horns, 128–29
Nuts
    Butterfinger Cupcakes, 154–55
    Caramel Pecan Bars, 133
    Chocolate-Hazelnut Lunch Box Tarts, 161
    Haystacks, 179
    Peanut Butter and Jelly Milk Shakes, 171

O

Outpost Popcorn Mix (Spicy Popcorn and
    Sweet Popcorn), 166–67

P

Pacific Wharf, Disney California Adventure
    Bavarian Pretzels, 223–24
Pandora—The World of Avatar, Disney's Animal Kingdom
    about: creation of, 187; food challenges,
      189
    Blueberry Cream Cheese Mousse, 185–87
    Cheeseburger Steamed Pods, 182–83
    Night Blossoms, 180–81
    Pongu Lumpia, 188
Pans, 34, 35, 37, 38, 41
Paper grocery bags, 39
Paradise Gardens Park, Disney California
    Adventure, Corn Dogs, 215
Parchment paper, 39
Passion Fruit Curd, 186
Peppers
    Roasted Jalapeño and Garlic Hummus, 64
    Roasted Red Pepper and Feta Hummus,
      63–64
Perfect Popcorn, 152
Peter Pan Floats, 101
Pineapple
    Blue Milk, 165
    Chocolate-Caramel Pineapple Spears, 132
    Dole Whip, 109
    Jungle Juleps, 61
    Mangonada Smoothies, 205
    Pineapple Upside Down Cake, 110
    Pongu Lumpia, 188
Piping bags, 39–40
Pixar Pier, Disney California Adventure
    Chicken Drumsticks, 216
    Chili-Lime Corn on the Cob, 217

Jack-Jack's Num Num Cookies, 218–19
Pixar Pier Frosty Parfaits, 221
Señor Buzz's Caliente Churros, 222
Pizza Spring Rolls, 107
Pongu Lumpia, 188
Popcorn. *See* Corn and popcorn
Popsicles. *See* Ice cream and frozen treats
Pork
    Bacon Macaroni & Cheese Hot Dogs, 87
    Carnitas Tacos, 206–7
    Chocolate-Hazelnut Lunch Box Tarts, 161
    French Fries with Pulled Pork and Cheese, 195
    Pork Belly Skewers, 65
    Ronto Wraps, 169–70
    Safari Skewers, 66
Potatoes
    French Fries with Pulled Pork and Cheese, 195
    Haystacks, 179
    Loaded Buffalo Chicken Tots, 104–5
    Mr. Kamal's Seasoned Fries, 189
Pots and pans, 41
Pressure cooker, 36
Pretzels
    Bavarian Pretzels, 223–24
    Mickey Pretzels, 158–60
    Pretzels with Cream Cheese Filling, 156–57
Pumpkin Spice Churros, 210

R

Ramekins, 41
Raspberries. *See* Berries
Recipes. *See also specific Disney Parks; specific food categories; specific main ingredients*
    about: overview of this book and, 16–17, 19, 21, 47
    getting started, 45
    tools for making. *See* Cooking essentials
Rolling pin, 41
Ronto Wraps, 169–70

S

Safari Skewers, 66
Sally's Summer Churros, 225–26
Sandwiches. *See also* Hot dogs
    Carnitas Tacos, 206–7
    Cheeseburger Steamed Pods, 182–83
    Ronto Wraps, 169–70
    Sweet-and-Spicy Chicken Waffle Sandwiches, 89–90
Sandwiches, sweet
    Fresh Fruit Waffle Sandwiches, 93
    Macaron Ice Cream Sandwiches, 118
Sauces
    Peppercorn Sauce, 169
    Spicy-Sweet Sauce, 90
Savory snacks and main dishes. *See also* Hot dogs; Sandwiches; Soups and chili; Waffles
    Baked Lobster Macaroni & Cheese, 199
    Baked Macaroni & Cheese with Pulled Pork, 196–98
    Bavarian Pretzels, 223–24
    Bengal Beef Skewers, 60
    Cheeseburger Steamed Rolls, 106
    Chicken Drumsticks, 216
    Chili-Lime Corn on the Cob, 217
    Crêpes, 123
    French Fries with Pulled Pork and Cheese, 195
    Loaded Buffalo Chicken Tots, 104–5
    Mickey Pretzels, 158–60
    Mr. Kamal's Seasoned Fries, 189
    Pork Belly Skewers, 65
    Safari Skewers, 66
    Tiger Tail Breadsticks, 62
    Turkey Legs, 103
School Bread, 127
Seafood
    Baked Lobster Macaroni & Cheese, 199
    Clam Chowder, 71
Señor Buzz's Caliente Churros, 222
Shaved ice maker, 42

Sieve/sifter, 42
Skewers
    about: wooden and soaking before using, 45
    Bengal Beef Skewers, 60
    Pork Belly Skewers, 65
    Safari Skewers, 66
Smoothies, 205, 208
S'mores, 212
Snacks, savory. *See* Hot dogs; Sandwiches; Savory snacks and main dishes; Soups and chili; Waffles
Snacks, sweet. *See* Churros; Cookies, cakes, and cupcakes; Desserts and sweet snacks; Ice cream and frozen treats; Waffles
Soups and chili
    Campfire Chili, 211
    Clam Chowder, 71
    Tomato Basil Soup, 102
Springform pan, 43
Stand mixer, 43
Star Wars: Galax's Edge, Disney's Hollywood Studios
    Blue Milk, 165
    Green Milk, 163–64
    Outpost Popcorn Mix (Spicy Popcorn and Sweet Popcorn), 166–67
    Ronto Wraps, 169–70
Steamer basket, 44
Stracciatella Gelato, 143
Strawberries. *See* Berries
Sunset Boulevard, Disney's Hollywood Studios
    Candy Apples, 151
    Perfect Popcorn, 152
Sweet-and-Spicy Chicken Waffle Sandwiches, 89–90

T

Tacos, carnitas, 206–7
Tarte aux Fraises, 124–26
Thermometers, 44
Tiger Tail Breadsticks, 62
Toffee, churro, 209
Tomato Basil Soup, 102
Tomorrowland, Disneyland, Brownie Bites, 79
Toy Story Land, Disney's Hollywood Studios
    Chocolate-Hazelnut Lunch Box Tarts, 161
    Lemon-Blueberry Lunch Box Tarts, 162
Troll Horns, 128–29
Turkey Legs, 103

W

Waffles
    Fresh Fruit Waffle Sandwiches, 93
    Mickey Waffles, 178
    Sweet-and-Spicy Chicken Waffle Sandwiches, 89–90
Wooden skewers, 45

About the Author

As a child who grew up in Anaheim Hills, California, Ashley Craft could recite the Star Tours ride by heart and navigate the park without a map, and fell asleep to the sound of Disneyland fireworks each night in her bedroom. After two internships at Walt Disney World and many, many more visits to the Disney Parks, Ashley is now one of the leading experts on Disneyland and Walt Disney World. Her popular blog, *Ashley Crafted*, is best known for featuring recipes inspired by Disney Park foods to help people re-create that Disney magic right in their own kitchens. Today, Ashley lives in Kansas with her husband, Danny, and three kids, Elliot, Hazel, and Clifford…but she still makes time to visit the Mouse. Learn more at AshleyCrafted.com.

Even More Magical Reads...

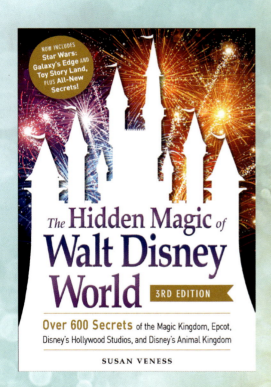
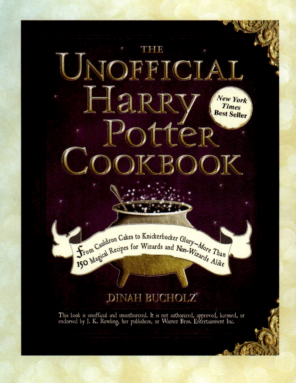

PICK UP OR DOWNLOAD YOUR COPIES TODAY!